KU-497-550

# Contents

# Introduction

*The Merchant of Venice* has fascinated and intrigued audiences and critics ever since Shakespeare wrote it some time around 1597. The play brilliantly fuses together a host of dramatic elements. It contains romantic courtship, riddling love tests, eloping lovers, comic confusions and a seemingly harmonious final act. There is an intensely gripping courtroom trial. Appearances are rarely what they seem: gold and silver prove to be worthless, identities are mistaken, women disguised as men trick their husbands.

But such features only partly explain why the play has so successfully stood the test of time. At its core is Shylock and his relentless pursuit of his bond. The pound of flesh that he seeks has made *The Merchant of Venice* the most contentious of all Shakespeare's plays, generating inflamed and passionate debate.

Shylock appears in only five of the 20 scenes but his presence dominates the play. The complexity of his character has been increasingly acknowledged. His moving plea for the common humanity of all races has become central to interpretations: 'Hath not a Jew eyes?' He has been accorded dignity, and seen as much as victim as villain. The same process of re-evaluation has acknowledged the anti-Semitism of his Christian tormentors and the corrosive mercantilism that pervades Venice. Even Belmont is no longer seen as a tranquil haven, but tinged with malign qualities that disfigure it.

Today no audience can watch a performance unaware of the brutal horrors of the Nazi persecution of the Jews. More than half a century after the Holocaust, the play still presents acutely troubling problems which have made it impossible to regard it as a simple comedy with a happy ending.

But the unsettling elements of the play are both a challenge and an opportunity. This guide will help you shape your responses to the rich diversity of language and subject matter, and to the oppositions that underpin the drama: Jew against Christian, love against hate, usury against venture trading, mercy against justice. The myriad of complex questions the play raises have no comforting or easy answers, but they will hugely reward your attention.

Cambridge Student Guide

Shakespeare

The Merchant
of Venice

Rob Smith

Series Editor: Rex Gibson

CAMBRIDGE
UNIVERSITY PRESS

PUBLISHED BY THE PRESS SYNDICATE OF THE UNIVERSITY OF CAMBRIDGE
The Pitt Building, Trumpington Street, Cambridge, United Kingdom

CAMBRIDGE UNIVERSITY PRESS
The Edinburgh Building, Cambridge CB2 2RU, UK
40 West 20th Street, New York, NY 10011–4211, USA
477 Williamstown Road, Port Melbourne, VIC 3207, Australia
Ruiz de Alarcón 13, 28014 Madrid, Spain
Dock House, The Waterfront, Cape Town 8001, South Africa

http://www.cambridge.org

© Cambridge University Press 2002

First published 2002

Printed in the United Kingdom at the University Press, Cambridge

*Typeface* 9.5/12pt Scala      *System* QuarkXPress®

*A catalogue record for this book is available from the British Library*

ISBN 0 521 00816 6 paperback

Cover image: © Getty Images/PhotoDisc

# Commentary

## Act 1 Scene 1

'In sooth I know not why I am so sad.' Antonio's first words quickly establish his melancholy mood at the opening of the play. They also show he is puzzled by his sadness. He does not know where it comes from, only that it wearies him. It makes him a stranger to himself: 'And such a want-wit sadness makes of me, / That I have much ado to know myself.' Just as Antonio is perplexed by his melancholy, so the nature and cause of his sadness will be a recurring puzzle for the audience throughout the play.

But Salarino and Solanio are in no doubt about the reasons for Antonio's melancholy. They think he is concerned about his commercial fortunes. Their witty speeches reveal much about Venice. It was renowned in Elizabethan times as a centre for trade and business. Its wealth and commercial activity are reflected in Salarino's claim that Antonio is worried about his merchant ships:

> your argosies with portly sail
> Like signors and rich burghers on the flood           *(lines 9–10)*

The language and imagery of Antonio's friends is extravagant and flamboyant. It hints at the wealthy Venetians' opulence and how their way of life is underpinned by trade and profit. Solanio describes the anxious behaviour he would display if he had money invested in such a risky enterprise. Salarino also attributes Antonio's sadness to worldly concerns. In a fanciful comparison, he claims that even if he went to church, the stone walls would remind him of shipwreck-causing rocks.

Antonio denies that his sadness is caused by concerns for his wealth. His quick denial of Solanio's jibe that he must be in love ('Fie, fie!') gives the actor a rich opportunity to suggest Antonio's troubled emotional state and to hint at the powerful motivations that lie behind his abrupt dismissal of love as a cause of his sadness. Solanio's response, that Antonio's sadness is surely due to his nature, may be spoken mockingly, but on stage the actor often delivers the lines affectionately, to suggest warm friendship.

The entry of Bassanio and his two friends, Lorenzo and Gratiano, is sometimes used in productions to suggest tensions between the young men. Their exchanges can be played in a friendly manner, or with thinly-veiled hostility. For example, Bassanio's line 'You grow exceeding strange' can be spoken with a smile or a sneer. But Shakespeare continues to keep attention focused on Antonio's melancholy. Gratiano also attributes the merchant's sadness to commercial concerns: 'You have too much respect upon the world'. When Antonio asserts that his role is to play a sad part in the world, Gratiano offers to play the fool. He embarks upon a long speech which satirises the fashionable melancholy affected by many Elizabethan men.

Following Gratiano's departure, the scene undergoes a change of mood. The young men's joking style gives way to an intimate and heartfelt exchange between Antonio and Bassanio. Once again, the Venetians' consuming preoccupation with wealth is evident. Bassanio catalogues his debts and confesses to having spent wildly beyond his means. His speech resonates with the language of money: 'estate', 'means', 'rate', 'debts', 'gaged', 'owe', 'warranty'. Antonio offers everything to help his friend:

> My purse, my person, my extremest means
> Lie all unlocked to your occasions.          *(lines 137–8)*

Antonio's offer will prove ominously prophetic as his 'person' will be fatally threatened by the bond that will be set up to guarantee Bassanio's spending. Productions often take Antonio's eager willingness to grant Bassanio anything as the opportunity to portray his strong homoerotic feelings for the younger man. Such portrayals suggest that this latent homosexual attraction is the cause of his melancholy. Other readings interpret this episode differently. They see it as Shakespeare signifying the powerful male friendship that will be evident throughout the play. Relying on that friendship, Bassanio sets out his plan. He needs money to finance his courtship of a rich and attractive young woman:

> In Belmont is a lady richly left,
> And she is fair, and – fairer than that word –
> Of wondrous virtues.          *(lines 160–2)*

Bassanio's fulsome praise of Portia uses extravagant comparisons. She is like another Portia, wife of the honourable Roman politician, Brutus. Bassanio's amorous pursuit of her is akin to the legendary seeking of the Golden Fleece (see page 62). She is 'fair' – a word that will resonate through the play. Perhaps most significantly, Portia is 'a lady richly left': she has inherited great riches. She therefore offers the means to clear Bassanio's debts if she becomes his wife.

There is telling irony in Bassanio's prediction that he will make a great profit: 'I have a mind presages me such thrift'. Antonio willingly agrees to finance Bassanio's journey to Belmont to woo Portia, but, aware that his money is tied up in his trading ventures, he suggests that Bassanio must use Antonio's reputation to secure credit to pay for his courtship of Portia. At the end of Scene 1, the issues of love and money are mixed together in a way which threatens dangerous consequences. That threat will become very real in Scene 3, when Antonio agrees his hazardous bond with Shylock.

## Act 1 Scene 2

Ironically, Portia's opening words echo Antonio's at the start of Scene 1. Both are 'aweary of this great world', Antonio because of sadness, Portia because of the arbitrary way in which she is bound by her dead father's will. Not only are the speeches counterpointed, so too are the locations. Shakespeare has moved the setting from commercial, business-fixated Venice to idealised and romantic Belmont (beautiful mountain), a name invented by Shakespeare for the purposes of the play. Belmont suggests a place of grace, refinement and elegance. A sea-voyage distant, it stands in marked contrast to Venice.

In Scene 1, designers decide how their sets might evoke the hard-edged, financial values of Venice. Now, in Scene 2, they usually strive to make Portia's home appear strikingly different. In the nineteenth and early twentieth century, productions attempted to create realistic settings with elaborate scenery. For example, Belmont could be a stately home with spacious, sweeping grounds and serene, dignified interiors. More recent productions often opt for unlocalised or symbolic settings, using costumes, lighting and a few simple props to help establish an appropriate mood. The shift of scene is also signified in the change from verse to prose. Although Portia is high status, she speaks prose, perhaps because Shakespeare judged the scene to be comic (see page 86).

There is an ironic tone to the whole scene. Although she is mistress of Belmont's immense wealth, Portia's freedom is strictly limited. She is bound by her dead father's will, and cannot even follow Nerissa's advice that it is better to exist with just enough money to live on. Her father's influence lives on beyond the grave. Portia will be given a husband in what seems an extreme form of an arranged marriage. Belmont may have a woman at its head, but it is still a patriarchal world.

Nerissa explains the terms of the will. Three caskets of gold, silver and lead offer Portia's suitors the chance to win her hand in marriage. Whoever solves the riddle of the inscriptions on the caskets and finds her portrait in one of them has the right to marry her. Since Portia is a rich and beautiful woman, it is not surprising that she has a string of suitors. But Shakespeare's presentation of Portia is complex. She may gain audience sympathy as a daughter constrained by the will of her father, and her comments on her suitors may evoke laughter, but she refers to them with damning scorn, and seems casually racist about their nationalities:

- The Neapolitan Prince is a 'colt', obsessed with horses.
- The County Palatine is too sad and melancholy.
- The Frenchman merely copies people and has no personality: 'he is every man in no man.'
- The Englishman is uneducated, and dresses and behaves badly.
- The Scotsman is a brawler.
- The German is a drunkard.

Portia's ridicule is masked behind comic stereotyping which probably reflects widely shared Elizabethan attitudes to foreigners. As will become clear, her dismissal of those outside her own society is an example of the intolerance that typifies the Christians in the play.

Portia's situation creates dramatic tension. She despises each of her suitors, but cannot refuse to marry the one who correctly solves the puzzle set by her father's will. Portia, trapped, compares herself to the chaste goddess Diana. She will die a virgin rather than renege on the conditions. But Shakespeare immediately offers a glimpse of a way out of her dilemma as Nerissa reminds her of Bassanio. On stage, Portia often reacts with obvious interest and enthusiasm to Nerissa's praise of Bassanio, suggesting she is half in love with him already.

But Portia has a pressing problem. The Prince of Morocco has arrived to seek her as his bride. Her response suggests that prejudice and bigotry lie beneath the outwardly 'fair' appearance of Belmont and its mistress:

> If he have the condition of a saint, and the complexion of a
> devil, I had rather he should shrive me than wive me.
>
> *(lines 106–8)*

## Act 1 Scene 3

Shakespeare's playwriting skill ensures that each scene is dramatically juxtaposed in some way to the scene that precedes it. Here, Portia's description of Morocco at the end of Scene 2 as having 'the complexion of a devil' may be a sinister preparation for the entry of Shylock. Like Morocco, he is an outsider, and will experience similar intolerant dismissal.

SHYLOCK   Three thousand ducats, well.
BASSANIO   Ay, sir, for three months.
SHYLOCK   For three months, well.
BASSANIO   For the which, as I told you, Antonio shall be bound.
SHYLOCK   Antonio shall become bound, well.          *(lines 1–5)*

Shylock's first words are about money: 'Three thousand ducats, well.' The line, and the dialogue that follows, shows that Bassanio is negotiating the loan to finance his courtship of Portia, and is using Antonio as security. Their conversation establishes a central motif of the play, the 'bond' between Antonio and Shylock. Shakespeare's concern for dramatic parallels is again evident. When Bassanio talks of Antonio being 'bound' by the terms of the loan, there are strong echoes of Portia's contractual obligation to the conditions laid down by her father. The bond and the caskets are thematically related.

The dialogue between Shylock and Bassanio bristles with mistrust. They spar verbally in tension-packed lines, repeating and echoing words: 'three', 'well' and 'bound'. When Shylock declares 'Antonio is a good man', he means that Antonio is 'sufficient': financially sound rather than decent or virtuous. In performance, Shylock often appears to savour every word and moment. He manipulates the dialogue, toying in cat-and-mouse fashion with Bassanio.

Shylock is a Jew in a Christian society which regards him and his race with ill-disguised or open contempt. He evidently enjoys the power he has at this moment. He has money, and so can finance a loan to one of the Christians who detest him. This is a rare moment of superiority, and Shakespeare provides him with language in which he can experience pleasure as he delays giving a decision. In contrast, Bassanio's frustrations are encapsulated in taut questions:

> May you stead me? Will you pleasure me? Shall I know your
> answer? *(lines 6–7)*

Bassanio's urgent questions convey his dislike of Shylock and the awkwardness he feels as a Christian having to ask a Jew for money. The hypocrisy that riddles Venetian society is clear. Bassanio despises Shylock but will use the Jew's money to fund his courtship of Portia.

The meeting takes place on the Rialto, the commercial centre of Venice, where deals are done and business gossip is exchanged. Evidence of that gossip is revealed in Shylock's detailed knowledge of Antonio's business ventures. He makes a little joke, punning on 'rats' and 'pirates' (which usually in performance adds to Bassanio's irritation). But there are hints of danger beneath the surface humour and the catalogue of Antonio's ships trading to faraway countries. All are ominous reminders of the perils of Antonio's ventures.

Shylock agrees to the loan, but he again toys with the meaning of words, repeating Bassanio's 'assured' with double emphasis. As Bassanio invites Shylock to dine with the Christians, the clash of cultures and religions is made sharply evident. Shylock will do business with the Christians but will not mix with them socially. Whether his lines are jokingly or seriously delivered, they confirm the gulf between their respective beliefs:

> I will buy with you, sell with you, talk with you, walk with
> you, and so following; but I will not eat with you, drink with
> you, nor pray with you. *(lines 28–30)*

Up to this point, the dialogue has been in prose. It switches to verse as Antonio enters. Shylock's dramatic aside expresses his hatred of Antonio and the Christians, reveals a financial reason for his hatred, and threatens ill for the Merchant:

> How like a fawning publican he looks!
> I hate him for he is a Christian;
> But more, for that in low simplicity
> He lends out money gratis, and brings down
> The rate of usance here with us in Venice.
> If I can catch him once upon the hip,
> I will feed fat the ancient grudge I bear him.     *(lines 33–9)*

Shylock's hate springs from Antonio's practice of lending money without charging interest. This hits Shylock's business profits hard because it reduces the rate of interest ('usance') he can charge on loans. He hopes to catch Antonio at a vulnerable moment, and so satisfy the long-standing enmity he feels towards him. Shylock goes on to say that Antonio hates all Jews and humiliates Shylock personally on the Rialto, where his day-to-day business is done. Shylock values his reputation amongst the merchants. To Shylock, his profits are 'well-won thrift' achieved by his financial skill. To Antonio they are purely 'interest', and therefore demeaning, sullied and uncharitable (see page 69). Forgiving Antonio is out of the question.

Shylock's aside carries all the force and energy of a revealing soliloquy. On stage, it is often delivered against a backdrop of Christian impatience. That impatience is exacerbated as Shylock (deliberately?) hesitates, pondering and 'debating of my present store'. Since Shylock has limited cash available to him at that moment, he will ask another wealthy Jew, Tubal, to subsidise the loan.

Shakespeare pointedly contrasts the motivations of Shylock and Antonio in the transaction. Antonio makes it clear that he disapproves of making profit from borrowing, but he will now make an exception to aid his friend Bassanio. Shylock justifies his ways of doing business by telling an involved biblical story about Jacob looking after Laban's sheep. Jacob's ingenuity led to considerable profit for himself. Shylock is proud to endorse this heritage and enterprise, although Antonio is clearly irritated by the detail and substance of the tale. Shylock's insistence that 'thrift is blessing' strongly links religion and profit. He is proud of his boast that he can multiply his wealth as quickly as Jacob's sheep bred in the story. Antonio's impatience bursts out in his disdain for people who act like devils, using biblical stories for their benefit:

The devil can cite Scripture for his purpose.
An evil soul producing holy witness
Is like a villain with a smiling cheek,
A goodly apple rotten at the heart.
O what a goodly outside falsehood hath!                    *(lines 90–4)*

The Christians' suspicion is powerfully demonstrated, encapsulated in the striking, condemnatory image of Shylock as the 'villain
with a smiling cheek'. It is a clear reference to the dangers which
Antonio thinks Shylock poses. Phrases such as 'evil soul' and 'rotten
at the heart' reveal Antonio's contempt for the Jew. But does Shylock
hear the words? That decision is made by each director of the play
(who may have Shylock choosing not to hear). On stage Shylock often
seems to talk to himself, musing on 'three thousand ducats' and the
rate of interest. Even his word 'rate' may be intended to further irritate
Antonio.

When Antonio asks directly if Shylock will loan the money, Shylock
responds passionately. Although Antonio has frequently insulted him
about his activities, Shylock has tolerated it patiently: Jews have
become accustomed to stoical endurance, wearing it like a 'badge'.
Antonio has labelled him 'misbeliever', 'cut-throat dog', spat on him
and kicked him, simply because he lent his money at interest. Shylock
mocks Antonio's small-minded hypocrisy. The very character who has
spat into his face now feels unabashed about using him as a money-
lender. Antonio does not have the grace or sensitivity to see him as
anything better than a stray dog, to be physically kicked around.
Shylock scornfully asks:

What should I say to you? Should I not say
'Hath a dog money? Is it possible
A cur can lend three thousand ducats?'                    *(lines 112–14)*

Shylock's heartfelt resentment and anger resonate through this
speech as he dominates the stage. The tension between the two
characters is already extreme, but Shakespeare allows a multitude of
possibilities for how Shylock might speak. He is seething inwardly,
but he might feign amused indifference. Alternatively, he might
overtly sneer at Antonio, or deliver a whining imitation of how he
might reply. In a scornful conclusion he asks if he should continue to

humble himself, begging like a slave to offer Antonio money as a token of his gratitude for being spurned.

Shylock's taunting parody brings a heated response. Antonio's reply bristles with contempt and arrogance. He will not change his deeply prejudiced attitude to Shylock and his money-lending ways. Friends do not profit at each other's expense. The money he requests should only be lent to an 'enemy', and if Antonio fails to repay, Shylock may exact the full penalty, whatever that may be:

> I am as like to call thee so again,
> To spit on thee again, to spurn thee too.
> If thou wilt lend this money, lend it not
> As to thy friends, for when did friendship take
> A breed for barren metal of his friend?
> But lend it rather to thine enemy,
> Who if he break, thou mayst with better face
> Exact the penalty. *(lines 122–9)*

In the face of such open hostility, Shylock seems to back down. He claims he wishes for friendship and love. As a gesture of goodwill, he will charge no interest on the loan, but offers, out of 'kindness' (a deeply ambiguous word), a 'merry sport'. The bond will be a 'pound of flesh'. If Antonio fails to repay, Shylock may cut the flesh from any part of Antonio's body that he chooses. For Elizabethan audiences the bond is rooted in deeply-held Christian fears and prejudices about the Jewish practice of circumcision (see page 68). An intriguing puzzle is posed for audiences across the ages: was the 'pound of flesh' in Shylock's mind before this moment, or is it a spur-of-the-moment decision?

Antonio immediately accepts the bond. Bassanio protests, but Antonio insists, expecting at least 'thrice three times' the required sum to be available at the appropriate time. Shylock mocks the Christians, blaming their suspicions on the mistrust their own harsh business practices have taught them. He argues that a pound of man's flesh is less valuable than a pound of animal meat. At this moment all productions have to decide how to present Shylock. Is he expressing genuine friendship? Or should the actor suggest by non-verbal dramatic action that Shylock has malign intentions in mind? Both interpretations have been frequently performed on stage.

As Shylock exits, he talks of speeding to the lawyer's chamber ('forthwith', 'straight', 'presently') as if he cannot wait to sign the contract. Antonio is pleased at the deal he has struck, even anticipating that Shylock's 'kind' gesture hints at a possible future conversion to Christianity. Yet again 'kind' is ambiguous, overtly meaning 'generous', but also implying 'like his kin, the Jews' (whose nature the Christians distrusted).

There are disturbing undercurrents beneath the fragile truce between the two religious factions in the play. Bassanio reminds Antonio that even though they have achieved fair and favourable terms for the bond, they should harbour suspicions about the 'villain' who has contrived it. But since Bassanio is so heavily in debt and relies desperately on Antonio as his patron, it is difficult for him to argue with Antonio's confidence and optimism, expressed in the concluding couplet of the act:

> Come on, in this there can be no dismay,
> My ships come home a month before the day.     *(lines 173–4)*

## Act 1: Critical review

Act 1 establishes certain themes or motifs that will recur through the play: the seemingly very different worlds of Belmont and Venice; the antagonism of Christian and Jew; the dramatic device of the 'bond'; and the untrustworthy nature of outward appearance.

Venice is a world of money and commerce. Bassanio must borrow cash to finance his quest to woo Portia. There is talk of usury (lending money at interest) and the contract of the bond that balances 3,000 ducats against a pound of vulnerable flesh. Venice is a masculine city, and the men are bound together by money.

In contrast, Belmont seems a feminine world of romance, trading only in love. It is ruled by a woman, Portia. But there are less benign features beneath the harmony and freedom Belmont seems to promise. Portia is bound by the will of her father. Patriarchy, not she herself, has decided how her husband shall be chosen. She must abide by the caskets test, but her remarks on her suitors suggest evidence of lurking racial prejudice in Belmont.

That prejudice is all too evident in Venice. Anti-Semitism balefully colours the relationships of Christians and Jews. Antonio is overtly contemptuous of Shylock. In return, Shylock loathes Antonio: 'I hate him for he is a Christian'.

In such a poisonous atmosphere, the bond that is struck between Antonio and Shylock clearly bodes ill. Shakespeare enables the actor playing Shylock to convince the audience that he has no malign intention in setting the forfeit as a pound of flesh. But even if the bond is a playful thought on Shylock's part, the festering animosity in Venice between Christian and Jew suggests that the drama will shortly take a sinister and destructive turn.

The suggestion that the comedy will take on a darker tone reveals another of the thematic preoccupations of Act 1: the disjunction of reality and appearance. It is obvious in Antonio's implicit characterisation of Shylock: 'a villain with a smiling cheek'. But Antonio's words have much wider application. Rich and successful Venice contains deepest prejudice. 'Fair' Portia's barbed comments suggest incipient racism. The caskets of gold, silver and lead may disguise secrets which contradict their outward appearance.

# Act 2 Scene 1

Act 2 returns to Belmont, where Morocco has arrived to try to win Portia. He is described in the stage direction as a 'tawny Moor', his dark skin creating a striking contrast with his white costume. Once more, there are sensitive issues of race to be considered as he asks Portia not to dislike him for his colour ('The shadowed livery of the burnished sun'). His language seems pompous and riddled with hyperbole, setting him up as a potential figure of hollowness and ridicule. Just as Shylock is an outsider in Venice, alienated by his faith and culture, so too is Morocco presented as an evident stranger in Belmont. His exaggerated self-justification of his colour suggests that intolerance and rejection will characterise Belmont as much as Venice.

Portia accepts that her personal choice has been replaced by 'the lottery of my destiny'. She seems critical of her dead father ('scanted me', 'hedged me') but is outwardly courteous to Morocco. But is she masking her real feelings for him behind an outward show of diplomacy and political correctness? Later, in Scene 7, her racist feelings towards him will become clear when she comments after he has chosen the wrong casket: 'Let all of his complexion choose me so.' But now she flatters him:

> Yourself, renownèd prince, then stood as fair
> As any comer I have looked on yet
> For my affection.
> 
> *(lines 20–2)*

Recalling her dismissive descriptions of her previous suitors, the audience may realise that she is not really praising Morocco! The language Shakespeare gives him hardly seems designed to help him win audience sympathy, but rather to create a stereotype of a boastful foreigner: an image Elizabethan audiences enjoyed and laughed at. He uses hyperbolic terms of action and daring to define his majesty: 'slew', 'o'er-stare', 'outbrave', 'pluck'. But even in his arrogance, Morocco displays a vulnerable side of his nature. He admits that Fortune (chance) may defeat his bid to win Portia, and he will 'die with grieving'. The price of failure is high. Portia's father has insisted that an unsuccessful suitor must never marry another woman. Dramatic tension escalates as the audience awaits Morocco's choice.

## Act 2 Scene 2

Scene 2 begins with Lancelot Gobbo's soliloquy. He imagines his
conscience and the devil are giving him different advice as to whether
he should leave Shylock. He never uses Shylock's name, but calls him
'the Jew'. In performance, the word is often spoken as a term of insult
and contempt. Lancelot's temptation to desert his master is
underpinned by his verdict that Shylock

> is a kind of devil . . . the Jew is the very devil incarnation
> *(lines 18–21)*

Elizabethan audiences are likely to have enjoyed Lancelot's
malapropism ('incarnation' instead of 'incarnate') and they almost
certainly laughed at Old Gobbo's encounter with Lancelot. Old Gobbo
is virtually blind and cannot recognise his son. Lancelot decides to
trick his father, convincing Old Gobbo that his son is dead. The
Elizabethans judged the dialogue and action as lively banter and
enjoyed the comic business. Today, audiences can find the scene
tedious or even cruel. In some productions it is cut altogether.

The old man has brought a present for Shylock, but Lancelot
persuades him to give it to Bassanio, who Lancelot hopes will employ
him as a servant. Lancelot explains that he has been starved by
Shylock's meanness, whereas in Bassanio's service he can expect 'rare
new liveries' (servants' uniforms). Once again, Venetian prejudice is
revealed in Lancelot's unpleasant use of 'Jew':

> My master's a very Jew . . . I am a Jew if I serve the Jew any
> longer.                                            *(lines 85–92)*

Old Gobbo gives his gift of doves to Bassanio, who accepts Lancelot
into his employment. Lancelot's words of thanks at lines 124–6 again
hint at the prejudice Christians in Venice feel for Jews. His proverb
suggests that Christians have 'the grace of God' whereas Shylock has
'enough' (wealth).

Bassanio is planning to depart for Belmont, and Gratiano implores
to be taken along. Bassanio agrees, but only if Gratiano mends his
behaviour, which is 'too wild, too rude, and bold of voice'. These are
not faults in the Venetian world, but are too vulgar and disruptive to
the elegant world of Belmont. Gratiano accepts the condition, but

probably mockingly as he describes the sober appearance he will adopt. Significantly, Bassanio urges Gratiano not to change his behaviour for that night's celebratory masque (a festivity involving music, dancing and feasting) in Venice. Some critics see hypocrisy in this apparently humorous episode. A studied deception is planned to ensure that, in Belmont, Gratiano's naturally raucous behaviour is concealed beneath a 'sober habit'. Nothing must spoil Bassanio's chances with Portia.

## Act 2 Scene 3

Lancelot's earlier criticism of Shylock's home is confirmed by Jessica, who gives a depressing picture of life there. Only Lancelot's joking lightens its gloom:

> Our house is hell, and thou a merry devil
> Didst rob it of some taste of tediousness.          *(lines 2–3)*

Jessica wants Lancelot to take a letter in secret to Lorenzo. Her soliloquy reveals she plans to marry Lorenzo and convert to Christianity. The short scene is dramatically important because it reveals that Shylock is rapidly becoming more isolated, rejected even by his own daughter. She feels ashamed to be his child. It also suggests Lancelot's genuine affection for Jessica: he weeps at the thought of leaving her. His warmth of feeling contrasts with Shylock's cold treatment of his daughter and concern for money. And, as in Belmont, there is no mention of a mother figure. Jessica, like Portia, is subject to her father's restrictions, but unlike her, plans to deceive him and escape.

## Act 2 Scene 4

The scene contains more examples of deception. The four Christians consider how they will disguise themselves to attend the masque. Jessica's letter reveals that she plans to disguise herself as a young male servant, and steal gold and jewels from her father as she elopes with Lorenzo.

It is uncertain to what extent the thought of gaining some of Shylock's money motivates Lorenzo. What is clear is that Jessica is abandoning her father and her religious heritage. Just as evident is the degree of Christian contempt for Shylock and his religion, expressed in Lorenzo's contrast of the Jew and his daughter:

If e'er the Jew her father come to heaven,
It will be for his gentle daughter's sake;
And never dare misfortune cross her foot,
Unless she do it under this excuse
That she is issue to a faithless Jew.                    *(lines 33–7)*

## Act 2 Scene 5

Shylock bids his servant a critical farewell, claiming that Lancelot has
eaten extravagantly and been lazy and careless in his service.
Reluctantly preparing to leave to dine with Bassanio, Shylock entrusts
the security of his house to Jessica, giving her the keys to his
home. Although he will eat with the Christians, he thinks they invite
him only to 'flatter' him. Nevertheless, he calculates that he will
at least be able to feed off the wasteful Christians. But he is
nervously apprehensive, and Shakespeare gives him a speech which
causes difficult problems for contemporary interpretations and
performances:

I am right loath to go;
There is some ill a-brewing towards my rest,
For I did dream of money bags tonight.                    *(lines 16–18)*

The difficulty lies in the final line. To Shakespeare's own audience,
Shylock's dream of money bags represented an ominous vision of
loss, not profit. In their view of Jews, it was an unexceptional remark,
merely confirming their prejudices (see pages 65–8). However, to
most modern ears the line sounds overtly anti-Semitic, because it
casts Shylock as the stereotypical money-obsessed Jew. Line 18 is often
cut in productions in order to avoid reducing the complexity of
Shylock's character.

Shylock is in sombre mood. The comic potential of Lancelot's
malapropism (saying Bassanio awaits his 'reproach' instead of his
'approach') fades as Shylock takes his words literally: he expects more
abuse from the Christians. Hearing that a masque is planned, Shylock
criticises the Christians' extravagance and exuberance. Once again
Shakespeare creates the possibility of seeing Shylock as a traditional
stereotype: the sour spoilsport opposed to harmless fun. He gives
strict orders to Jessica:

> Lock up my doors, and when you hear the drum
> And the vile squealing of the wry-necked fife,
> Clamber not you up to the casements then
> Nor thrust your head into the public street
> To gaze on Christian fools with varnished faces;   *(lines 28–32)*

This unsympathetic presentation of Shylock is extended through his obsession with keys and security. His 'sober house' becomes a locked fortress, a refuge safe from the noise of 'shallow foppery'. Perhaps Shakespeare, about to show Jessica's betrayal of her father, is encouraging the audience to see Shylock unsympathetically. That impression is strengthened as he again criticises Lancelot ('a huge feeder, / Snail-slow in profit'), hopes Lancelot will waste Bassanio's borrowed money, and leaves with an instruction to Jessica in the form of a snappy proverb about order, security and thrift: 'Fast bind, fast find'. Jessica's final rhyming couplet suggests that Shylock is about to suffer even more grievously than he could possibly anticipate:

> Farewell, and if my fortune be not crossed,
> I have a father, you a daughter, lost.   *(lines 54–5)*

## Act 2 Scene 6

Outside Shylock's house Gratiano and Salarino are surprised that Lorenzo is late when he should so eagerly be anticipating meeting Jessica. Both men talk of the greater pleasure in the first anticipation of love than in its actual experience. Gratiano uses language heavily steeped in sensations of physical enjoyment and satisfaction: 'keen appetite', 'unbated fire'. He even compares the winds in the sails of a ship to the embrace of a prostitute. These may be the kind of men who desire women physically, but don't like them very much. For Gratiano,

> All things that are
> Are with more spirit chasèd than enjoyed.   *(lines 13–14)*

The young men's passionate delight in immediate pleasure stands in marked opposition to Shylock's remarks about his 'sober house' in the previous scene. The contrast is made more obvious as Lorenzo engineers Jessica's elopement. She appears dressed as a boy, and exchanges mutual declarations of love with Lorenzo. But Jessica feels shame about her male disguise, and in one of the play's best-known lines, excuses her cross-dressing:

> But love is blind, and lovers cannot see
> The pretty follies that themselves commit;        *(lines 37–8)*

But this is Venice, and as well as the language of love and the romance of elopement, Shakespeare ensures that the calculating, commercial aspects of the city are evident. Jessica steals her own dowry, a casket of gold and jewels plundered from her father. But she is not content with what she has. She takes even more:

> I will make fast the doors, and gild myself
> With some moe ducats        *(lines 50–1)*

Jessica's betrayal of her roots and her father evokes admiration from Gratiano. He calls her 'a gentle' (a woman of refinement and manners) who is 'no Jew!' ('gentle' may also be seen as a pun on 'Gentile'). Shakespeare loads Lorenzo's admiration with an irony of which Lorenzo is unaware. A daughter has betrayed her father's trust, but in Lorenzo's eyes:

> And true she is, as she hath proved herself:
> And therefore like herself, wise, fair, and true        *(lines 56–7)*

## Act 2 Scene 7

The scene switches to Belmont, and the first of the casket scenes. Although Portia's opening words are clipped imperatives ('draw', 'discover', 'make') they imply that the business of choosing is a serious ceremony. In performance, the ritual disclosure of the casket and Morocco's approach are often staged with elaborate dignity. What the caskets are like (small ornaments? massive urns?), and how far Portia reveals her feelings about whether Morocco makes the correct choice, varies from production to production.

Morocco's lengthy speech as he explores the inscriptions on the caskets begins with a reference to pagan beliefs, which again confirms his 'outsider' status: 'Some god direct my judgement!' It continues in the same heightened and elaborate style he used in Act 2 Scene 1, as, for example, in his hyperbolic praise of Portia:

From the four corners of the earth they come
To kiss this shrine, this mortal breathing saint.
The Hyrcanian deserts and the vasty wilds
Of wide Arabia are as throughfares now
For princes to come view fair Portia.                    *(lines 39–43)*

Morocco's speech resonates with references to himself as he contemptuously dismisses the lead and silver caskets. It becomes more and more evident that he will choose by outward appearance. For him, Portia ('so rich a gem') can only be set in gold. As Morocco moves towards his choice, Shakespeare gives him a line about 'an angel' (an English gold coin) that would have specially appealed to his Elizabethan audience (see page 65). Predictably, Morocco chooses the gold casket, unlocks it, and finds inside not Portia's picture, but a skull. In the eye socket is the damning proverbial inscription:

'All that glisters is not gold;
Often have you heard that told.'                    *(lines 65–6)*

The crestfallen Morocco exits, and Portia bids him 'A gentle riddance!', barely able to contain her contempt. Her racism surfaces bitingly in her final line:

Let all of his complexion choose me so.                    *(line 79)*

## Act 2 Scene 8

The previous scene closed with one loser, Morocco. Now Scene 8 opens with the report of another loser, Shylock. Salarino and Solanio tell how Shylock responded to the loss of his daughter and his possessions. Some directors, perhaps disappointed with the fact that Shylock's despair is not witnessed directly, have added an extra scene, not written by Shakespeare, in which Shylock returns home to discover Jessica's betrayal. Such an addition can also have the effect of counterbalancing some of the undoubted prejudice and bigotry displayed in this scene, in which Shylock's actions are filtered through the Christians' distinctly hostile perception.

Once again, Shylock is not named. He is described as 'the villain Jew' and 'the dog Jew'. In allowing the Christians to report Shylock's plight, Shakespeare gives them licence to portray his grievances unsympathetically and unattractively. Solanio seems to take mocking pleasure in imitating (or claiming to imitate) Shylock, portraying him as equally concerned for his money and Jessica:

> 'My daughter! O my ducats! O my daughter!
> Fled with a Christian! O my Christian ducats!
> Justice! The law! My ducats and my daughter!'     *(lines 15–17)*

But even in Solanio's jeering imitation, the intensity of Shylock's anger is evident. His passions fluctuate between personal grief at the loss of his only close relative and of his possessions. And his sense of hurt at the betrayal has given rise to the demand for justice and revenge. Already he has lobbied and engaged the Duke of Venice in his search for Jessica and Lorenzo.

Salarino piles on cruel detail: even children delight in Shylock's suffering. They follow and taunt him, ridiculing his theatrical reactions and preying on his vulnerable emotions. But as the two Venetians talk, they realise that dangerous consequences might lie ahead for Antonio. The wounded and humiliated Shylock will be a dangerous adversary if Antonio fails to repay the bond. That prospect looms as Salarino recalls the report of a Venetian trading vessel shipwrecked in the English Channel.

In contrast to the marked hostility towards Shylock's plight displayed in the first half of the scene, the second half sees the two men voicing compassion and tenderness towards Antonio. There is a description of his touching farewell to Bassanio, wishing him all success in Belmont, and unable to hold back tears. Some critics interpret Solanio's words as revealing that Antonio's unfulfilled homoerotic feelings for Bassanio are the cause of his melancholy:

> I think he only loves the world for him.     *(line 51)*

## Act 2 Scene 9

In Belmont, Portia prepares to receive her second suitor, the Prince of Arragon. Once again there is opportunity for elaborate theatrical ceremony as Arragon and his followers enter and Portia begins the ritual of the caskets. Arragon makes it clear that he is 'enjoined by oath' to observe the conditions of his choice. He must never tell which casket he chooses; if he fails, he must never marry and he must leave immediately.

Arragon deliberates over his choice, showing greater wisdom than Morocco in admitting that many fools 'choose by show', their eyes unable to see what lies beneath outward appearance. But Arragon shares Morocco's arrogance, expressing his self-confidence in pompous bombast as he rejects the golden casket:

> I will not choose what many men desire,
> Because I will not jump with common spirits,
> And rank me with the barbarous multitudes.     *(lines 30–2)*

Arragon, full of self-importance, opts for the silver casket, with its inscription 'Who chooseth me, shall get as much as he deserves.' The inscription ironically proves him right as he unlocks the casket, and pauses at length as he discovers its contents:

> What's here? The portrait of a blinking idiot
> Presenting me a schedule!     *(lines 53–4)*

Arragon's couplets as he departs reveal that for all his previous bombast and self-assurance, he is fully aware of the implications of his failure, and intends to keep the vow he has sworn:

> With one fool's head I came to woo,
> But I go away with two.
> Sweet, adieu; I'll keep my oath,
> Patiently to bear my wroth.     *(lines 74–7)*

After Arragon has left, Portia mocks him as an insect ('Thus hath the candle singed the moth') and as yet another of the 'deliberate fools' who attempt to solve the caskets' riddles by excessive ('deliberate') reasoning. The scene could have ended here, but a messenger brings news of another visitor. A young Venetian messenger has arrived, telling that his master is coming to Belmont. The contrast between the inadequacies of the recent failed suitors and the promise of this new suitor is marked. If the young Venetian is 'A day in April' (spring) then he presages Bassanio, who is 'costly [splendid] summer'. Portia sarcastically dismisses the Messenger's praise of the newly arrived visitor. Her closing exchange displays her strong sense of irony, and Nerissa's hope that the suitor will be Bassanio:

PORTIA  Come, come, Nerissa, for I long to see
         Quick Cupid's post that comes so mannerly.
NERISSA  Bassanio, Lord Love, if thy will it be!    *(lines 98–100)*

## Act 2: Critical review

Throughout Act 2 Shakespeare's dramatic skills are evident as he juxtaposes scenes for theatrical effect. The rapid switches from location to location allow each scene to contrast vividly with the next, illuminating in different ways the themes of deceptive appearance and anti-Semitism.

The mismatch of reality and appearance occurs in many ways. Portia uses a veneer of courteous civility to conceal her true feelings for the 'tawny Moor' Morocco. Lancelot Gobbo cruelly deceives his father into believing his son is dead. Jessica plans to deceive her father. Later in the act she hides her gender in male garments.

Other scenes continue the theme of deception. The Christians disguise themselves in masks. Shylock warns Jessica of the foolishness that lies within Christian festivity. Salarino tells how Antonio tried to hide his feelings as he parted from Bassanio. Perhaps the motif of deceptive appearance is most memorably evident in the casket theme. Both Morocco and Arragon are deceived by outward appearance as they choose the gold and silver caskets.

But what is not concealed behind benign appearances is the anti-Semitism of the Christians. As they talk of Shylock they typically deny him his name. To Lancelot he is 'the Jew', 'the very devil', 'the rich Jew'. The high-status Christians take delight in mocking Shylock's grief for his daughter and his stolen money. To them he is 'villain Jew', 'dog Jew'.

The act shows the increasing isolation of Shylock, deserted by his servant and betrayed by his daughter. He loses audience sympathy for his harsh treatment of Jessica. He speaks a line (sometimes cut from modern productions) which promotes the stereotypical image of the greedy Jew: 'For I did dream of money bags tonight.' But in Scene 8, Shakespeare balances such negative characteristics against the vileness of the Christians' derisory imitation of Shylock's grief.

Shakespeare also ensures that love is prominent throughout the act. As Jessica elopes, she excuses her shame at dressing as a boy: 'But love is blind'. In the final scene, as Portia awaits Bassanio she hears the Messenger's lyrical report of his impending arrival: 'A day in April never came so sweet'.

# Act 3 Scene 1

Shakespeare continues his practice of juxtaposing scenes. The previous scene ended with the hope of love. This scene opens with fears for Antonio, and then develops with vehement expression of hate.

Solanio and Salarino discuss bad news about Antonio's trading ventures. One of his ships has been lost on the Goodwin Sands off the coast of England. The tone of their conversation is full of warmth for 'the good Antonio, the honest Antonio', but they express foreboding for his future. Neither man names Shylock, but it is obvious they feel he will harm Antonio, and Solanio makes their feelings evident as Shylock approaches:

> Let me say 'amen' betimes, lest the devil cross my prayer, for
> here he comes in the likeness of a Jew.          *(lines 17–18)*

Shylock clearly suspects that the two Christians are part of the conspiracy which organised Jessica's elopement. His language shows him to be hurt, humiliated, vulnerable – and very angry. The two Christians taunt him, utterly unsympathetic to the acute pain he feels at the loss of his daughter. They twist his words, hinting at his sexual impotence ('Rebels it at these years?'), and jibing that Shylock and Jessica are not of the same stock, but are quite different in nature.

As talk turns to Antonio's losses, Shylock bemoans the fact that he has struck a bargain with a 'bankrupt'. His threefold repetition of 'Let him look to his bond' becomes a menacing refrain. Shylock intends to pursue his bond to 'feed my revenge'. Actors playing Shylock sometimes heavily emphasise the word 'feed' to suggest the searing hunger for vengeance that Shylock feels gnawing away at him. The intensity of that feeling is evident in the outburst in which he lists a long catalogue of his grievances against Antonio, personal, financial and religious:

> He hath disgraced me, and hindered me half a million,
> laughed at my losses, mocked at my gains, scorned my nation,
> thwarted my bargains, cooled my friends, heated mine
> enemies          *(lines 43–5)*

The active verbs that Shylock uses ('disgraced', 'hindered', 'laughed at' and so on), all present Antonio as forcefully seizing every occasion to revile and obstruct him. 'And what's his reason?' demands Shylock. His reply to his own question has become one of the most famous statements of the common humanity of all races:

> I am a Jew. Hath not a Jew eyes? Hath not a Jew hands,
> organs, dimensions, senses, affections, passions? Fed with the
> same food, hurt with the same weapons, subject to the same
> diseases, healed by the same means, warmed and cooled by
> the same winter and summer as a Christian is? If you prick us,
> do we not bleed? If you tickle us, do we not laugh? If you
> poison us, do we not die?                              *(lines 46–52)*

Shylock's plea is heartfelt and deeply moving. The logic of his rhetorical questions is undeniable: all human beings share characteristics which make them human. The speech is dignified and passionate, profoundly simple and profoundly true. The effect in the theatre is usually to evoke deeply-felt audience sympathy. But as Shylock poignantly expresses his pain and bewilderment at his treatment, his rhetorical questions culminate in a chilling conclusion that justifies taking bloody revenge:

> And if you wrong us, shall we not revenge? If we are like you
> in the rest, we will resemble you in that.            *(lines 52–3)*

Shylock has learnt from Christian example: 'The villainy you teach me I will execute'. This seems to be the moment when Shylock's decision to pursue his revenge becomes absolute and immutable. Brutality has bred brutality, but Shylock vows to outdo the Christians in their villainy and detestation. That Christian contempt for Jews is once again made evident with the arrival of Tubal. Solanio scathingly remarks:

> Here comes another of the tribe; a third cannot be matched,
> unless the devil himself turn Jew.                    *(lines 61–2)*

Tubal provides one of the few insights in the play into the wider world of the Jews. It seems that Shylock has entrusted the task of tracing his daughter to Tubal, and he eagerly asks for information about her. In his travels, Tubal has often heard of Jessica, but has not found her. His words provoke Shylock to another violent outburst. Jessica's betrayal and desertion, and her theft of his wealth produce a lament that Elizabethan audiences may have found humorous because it confirmed their comic stereotype of a money-obsessed, heartless Jew. Today, however, audiences usually find his diatribe disconcerting, inhumane and savagely vindictive:

> I would my daughter were dead at my foot, and the jewels in
> her ear: would she were hearsed at my foot, and the ducats in
> her coffin. *(lines 69–71)*

Here, Shakespeare seems concerned to make it difficult to sympathise with Shylock, whose emotions swirl so wildly. His clipped sentences veer violently from thought to harrowing thought: the loss of diamonds and ducats, the desire for his daughter's death, the cost of the search ('loss upon loss'), and no possibility of satisfaction in revenge.

Shylock feels entirely alone in his grief: 'no tears but o'my shedding!' Tubal tries to ease his anguish, reporting that one of Antonio's ships has been wrecked. The news temporarily cheers Shylock. His short sentences and exclamations express triumph and delight. But Tubal's next words renew his torment. He is devastated to learn that Jessica has spent 'four score ducats' in one evening. Shylock's mood fluctuates agonisingly. The more he feels his losses, the more he is determined to have his revenge on Antonio. Hearing Tubal's news that Antonio's many creditors are certain he will become bankrupt, Shylock expresses his pleasure in short, venomous phrases:

> I am very glad of it. I'll plague him, I'll torture him. I am glad
> of it. *(lines 91–2)*

But Shakespeare now reveals an aspect of Shylock's character which suggests his emotional vulnerability and a loving past. He learns from Tubal that Jessica has exchanged a precious ring for a frippery – a monkey. The news touches a tender chord, as the ring held great sentimental value for Shylock:

> Thou torturest me, Tubal: it was my turquoise, I had it of Leah
> when I was a bachelor. I would not have given it for a
> wilderness of monkeys.                                    *(lines 95–7)*

Who was Leah? Perhaps she was Shylock's wife. Shakespeare gives
his response a poignancy that can cause audiences to revise their
unsympathetic judgement of Shylock's character. In the theatre, his
words can be powerfully affecting. For example, Laurence Olivier gave
the final phrase particular resonance by delivering it with a howl of
anguish. But the scene closes with Shylock intent on pursuing
Antonio. He gives the order for an officer to arrest him, and speaks
words expressing ominous malice if Antonio cannot repay the bond:

> I will have the heart of him if he forfeit          *(lines 100–1)*

# Act 3 Scene 2

After a scene of hate, a scene of love. This third casket scene reveals
how very differently Portia treats Bassanio from her other suitors. In
the earlier courtship scenes she was relatively passive. Now she holds
the stage with a long speech before Bassanio makes his choice. Her
previous arrogance, confidence and contempt are no longer evident.
In contrast to how she urged her other two suitors to choose, and
relished their departure, she now implores Bassanio to forbear from
making his choice immediately.

Portia's words seem softer, her sentences longer and more
reflective, littered with uncertainties and doubts as she struggles with
her hopes and fears. She wants to tell Bassanio which casket to
choose, but she cannot break her vow to her father never to reveal
the secret. Her hesitation and nervous anticipation are typical signs
of someone in love, and she clearly declares her affection for
Bassanio:

> One half of me is yours, the other half yours –
> Mine own, I would say: but if mine then yours,
> And so all yours.                                    *(lines 16–18)*

The length, style and content of Portia's speech creates dramatic
tension. That tension becomes the subject of an image as Bassanio
compares his waiting to the agony of being 'upon the rack': an

instrument of torture which stretched its victims' limbs. Shakespeare extends this torture metaphor in the dialogue that follows. It ranges over ideas of treason and confession, and Portia uses it to test the integrity of Bassanio's love. Some critics argue that here Shakespeare is reminding the audience that Bassanio's love might not be as pure as he claims, and is motivated by thoughts of Portia's fortune. But the extended image ends with Bassanio insisting he has only love in mind: "Confess and love".

Portia orders the ceremony of choice to begin. She declares that if Bassanio's love is true, he will choose correctly. She calls for music, and uses the image of music to make elaborate comparisons (see pages 81–2): if he loses, Bassanio is like a swan dying upon her river of tears; if he succeeds, it is like a fanfare for a monarch, or music that wakes a bridegroom on his wedding day. She compares herself to a helpless sacrificial virgin rescued by Alcides (Hercules) from a sea monster, and directly addresses Bassanio as that legendary hero ('Go, Hercules!'), ordering him to make his choice.

The song that accompanies Bassanio's inspection of the caskets may be Shakespeare's device to avoid having the casket inscriptions read aloud yet again. But the song's meaning is also dramatically significant because it warns against the danger of superficial appearances. Some critics point to the strong rhyming hint carried in the song's first three lines. Each one rhymes with 'lead':

> Tell me where is fancy bred,
> Or in the heart, or in the head?
> How begot, how nourishèd?                    *(lines 63–5)*

Bassanio's choosing speech explores a key theme of the play, and indeed of every Shakespeare play – the disjunction between appearance and reality. Outward appearances can conceal quite different inner qualities: 'So may the outward shows be least themselves'. Bassanio uses graphic images to explore how appearances are deceptive and belie inner reality:

- Criminals can plead persuasively ('gracious voice') to disguise their sin.
- Quotations from holy books conceal religious transgressions ('damnèd error').

- Vice hides behind a show of virtue.
- Cowards pretend to be great warriors (such as Hercules or Mars).
- Outward beauty ('supposèd fairness') is achieved by cosmetics and wigs.
- 'Ornament' is like an attractive but treacherous shore beside a dangerous sea; like a beautiful scarf that hides an unattractive face. ('Indian beauty' is yet another example of the casual racist language of Elizabethan England, see page 36.)

Following the logic of his argument, Bassanio rejects the gold and silver caskets and chooses the casket of lead. Portia knows he has chosen correctly. Her fears vanish, and she is consumed with a passion of love and joy that threatens to overwhelm her:

> O love, be moderate, allay thy ecstasy,
> In measure rain thy joy, scant this excess!
> I feel too much thy blessing: make it less
> For fear I surfeit.                          *(lines 111–14)*

Bassanio's response to finding Portia's picture inside the lead casket is similarly extreme. You can find on page 82 a discussion of his extended conceit (a speech involving exaggerated and elaborate imagery) claiming that no words can do Portia full justice. The words on the scroll inside the casket confirm that success goes to the person who is not deceived by outward appearances:

> 'You that choose not by the view
> Chance as fair, and choose as true.'          *(lines 131–2)*

Bassanio kisses Portia, but feels unable to believe his good fortune until his engagement to her is 'confirmed, signed, ratified by you'. Critics point to the commercial nature of his language, and to the fact that this becomes the second contract in which Bassanio has been involved. Portia's response begins with utter simplicity ('You see me, Lord Bassanio, where I stand, / Such as I am'), but continues with the language of monetary wealth as she wishes her value increased for Bassanio ('ten thousand times / More rich'). In language which Elizabethans probably found unexceptional, but which has drawn the attention of feminist critics, she commits herself to Bassanio as 'her lord, her governor, her king', and gives everything she possesses to him:

> This house, these servants, and this same myself
> Are yours, my lord's. *(lines 170–1)*

Portia's submission to Bassanio is absolute, and she seals it with the gift of a love ring, declaring that if Bassanio gives the ring away, it will foretell the ruin of his love, and give her opportunity to denounce him loudly. This begins the 'rings' plot, which will have comic consequences. In fact, the comedy starts at once, with Gratiano's surprise announcement that he has successfully wooed Nerissa. His words celebrate the idea of love at first sight:

> You saw the mistress, I beheld the maid. *(line 198)*

Gratiano jokingly wagers that his son will be born before a son of Portia and Bassanio, but the briefly comic mood changes with the arrival of Lorenzo, Jessica and Salerio. Jessica's arrival in Belmont signifies a shift towards her conversion to Christianity. She is greeted as Lorenzo's 'infidel', a label which emphasises she is not a Christian and denies her the courtesy of her name. In some modern productions, Portia has coldly ignored Jessica, welcoming only the Christians.

Bassanio assumes his position of master of Belmont as he greets the new arrivals. But the colour drains from his cheek as he reads the letter from 'that royal merchant, good Antonio'. He tells Portia that Antonio financed his expedition to Belmont, but now his friend's trading ventures have failed entirely. Antonio's merchant vessels have all been shipwrecked. Salerio adds worse news. Shylock is pursuing Antonio remorselessly, appealing unceasingly to the Duke of Venice to grant him justice. He is deaf to the entreaties of all the hierarchy of Venice to release Antonio from his bond:

> Besides, it should appear that if he had
> The present money to discharge the Jew,
> He would not take it. Never did I know
> A creature that did bear the shape of man
> So keen and greedy to confound a man.

He plies the Duke at morning and at night,
And doth impeach the freedom of the state
If they deny him justice. Twenty merchants,
The Duke himself, and the magnificoes
Of greatest port have all persuaded with him,
But none can drive him from the envious plea
Of forfeiture, of justice, and his bond.          *(lines 271–82)*

Salerio, a Christian, typically portrays Shylock as an inhuman 'creature', greedy for Antonio's ruin. Significantly, that view is confirmed by Jessica, who tells that she has heard her father swearing he would rather have Antonio's flesh than a massive profit on the bond. Whether Jessica adds her damning detail eagerly or reluctantly poses a difficult challenge for the actress playing her. In one production she delivered her lines haltingly and barely audibly, forced into speech because the eyes of all the Christian characters turned accusingly on her. In another production she offered her news enthusiastically, apparently with the intention of ingratiating herself to the Christians (who responded by contemptuously ignoring her).

Counterpointing the debasing descriptions of Shylock as 'the Jew', Antonio is spoken of as 'dearest friend' and 'kindest man'. Portia proposes her solution: Bassanio must first marry her, but leave instantly for Venice and repay the bond, even paying 20 times the amount owed. He must then return to Belmont with his friend Antonio. Portia speaks with authority and great decisiveness, but there seems to be an uneasy balance between the worlds of money and love in her description of Bassanio:

Since you are dear bought, I will love you dear.          *(line 312)*

## Act 3 Scene 3

In Venice, Shylock has begun to exact his revenge. He has had Antonio arrested, and vehemently refuses mercy. Antonio will be threatened later by Shylock's real knife, but here Shylock twists the metaphorical knife by labelling Antonio a 'fool' for lending money without interest. He cuts short Antonio's attempt to speak, repeating forcefully that he will have his bond, and turning Antonio's previous abuse of him into a menacing image:

> Thou call'dst me dog before thou hadst a cause,
> But since I am a dog, beware my fangs. *(lines 6–7)*

Again Antonio attempts to speak, and again Shylock prevents him, repeating insistently 'I'll have my bond.' Shylock knows that the Duke must grant him justice, and after Shylock has left, Antonio acknowledges that will inevitably happen. Shylock wants him dead, especially as he has often financially rescued many debtors from Shylock's clutches. The wealth of Venice rests on trade, and to maintain the trust of foreign traders, the 'justice of the state' must take its course, upholding the rights of every citizen. Antonio knows it is pointless to plead with Shylock, and that tomorrow he must pay the bloody penalty. But the equally powerful bond of male friendship is evident as Antonio prays that as long as Bassanio is present at his death, he will be content:

> Well, jailer, on. Pray God Bassanio come
> To see me pay his debt, and then I care not. *(lines 35–6)*

## Act 3 Scene 4

The bond of intense male friendship that closed Scene 3 is the subject of the opening of Scene 4. Lorenzo praises Portia formally but extravagantly, especially for enabling Bassanio to help his friend Antonio: 'How dear a lover'. Portia replies in equally formal language, acknowledging Antonio as 'the bosom lover of my lord' and implying that two men who are so close share identical characteristics:

> Of lineaments, of manners, and of spirit *(line 15)*

She states that any amount she spends is too little to rescue someone so like Bassanio ('the semblance of my soul'), but then, rejecting self-indulgence, assumes a businesslike tone. She appoints Lorenzo as master of Belmont until Bassanio returns, and says that she plans to stay in a convent until that time. She responds directly to Jessica's good wishes, and their brief exchange gives a significant opportunity to show the nature of their relationship. Some productions show Portia displaying an icy disdain in her apparently courteous reply:

JESSICA   I wish your ladyship all heart's content.

PORTIA   I thank you for your wish, and am well pleased
       To wish it back on you: fare you well, Jessica.   *(lines 42–4)*

Portia despatches Balthazar with a letter to Doctor Bellario in Padua. She instructs Balthazar to bring the clothes and notes Bellario provides back to her at the ferry port for Venice. Alone with Nerissa, Portia reveals that her 'convent' plan is a deceit. She and Nerissa will disguise themselves as young men, and in that disguise will see their husbands in Venice. The theme of appearance and reality will recur in a different form. Portia's mocking of male behaviour suggests that she has an alert understanding of masculine habits and is well aware of the sexual implications of language:

NERISSA                Why, shall we turn to men?

PORTIA   Fie, what a question's that,
       If thou wert near a lewd interpreter!   *(lines 78–80)*

## Act 3 Scene 5

Shakespeare chooses to end Act 3 with a seemingly light-hearted domestic scene. Some critics dismiss it as unimportant, a 'filler' designed to give Portia and Nerissa time to change their costumes. But the scene has significant and troubling aspects. Lancelot's teasing of Jessica displays the Christian bigotry that assumes Jews are damned:

> Yes truly, for look you, the sins of the father are to be laid
> upon the children. Therefore I promise you I fear you. I was
> always plain with you, and so now I speak my agitation of the
> matter. Therefore be o'good cheer, for truly I think you are
> damned. There is but one hope in it that can do you any good,
> and that is but a kind of bastard hope neither.   *(lines 1–6)*

When Jessica reveals she has converted to Christianity, Lancelot's joke about 'pork eaters' conveys the casual racism of Elizabethan Christians towards Jews. There is similar racism in his punning response to Lorenzo's news that Lancelot has made a black woman pregnant. It prompts Lorenzo to a remark about the slipperiness of language that some critics believe expresses Shakespeare's own view:

How every fool can play upon the word! *(line 36)*

The scene shows no evidence of Tubal's damning indictments of Jessica's profligate spending, and it is often claimed to present the domestic harmony of Lorenzo and Jessica. However, the director Jonathan Miller transformed it into a scene which portrayed Lorenzo as a humourless, pompous prig, who treated Jessica like a small child. Whatever the characterisation of their relationship, Jessica's fulsome praise of Portia in the language of religious adoration might be interpreted as preparation for Portia's role in the crucial trial scene that follows.

## Act 3: Critical review

Hate and love alternate throughout the act. News of Antonio's shipwrecked trading vessels leads Shylock to rejoice that the Christian merchant now really is in his power. 'I'll torture him' he balefully threatens. In Scene 3 Antonio seems quite literally 'bound' by Shylock's arresting officer. All Shylock's venom and desire for revenge emerges with his repeated insistence: 'I'll have my bond'.

But Shakespeare's stagecraft balances loathing against love, and Bassanio wins the 'Golden Fleece': Portia. This casket scene explores further the crucial theme of reality and appearance. Portia's two earlier suitors, Morocco and Arragon, were beguiled by the outward show of the gold and silver caskets. But Bassanio's long speech as he makes his choice shows he is fully aware of the deluding power of appearance.

Bassanio's correct choice not only wins him Portia, but all she possesses, including Belmont. Patriarchal tendencies in Shakespeare's society are made all too evident, as Portia gives everything to her husband. Critical opinion varies widely on whether Shakespeare is endorsing or condemning such a show of female submission.

Shakespeare opposes one episode against another. Thus Portia gives Bassanio the ring which will later have humiliating consequences for him. She plans to dress in male clothes and challenge the men on their own ground. Her action is more than a cross-dressing dramatic device of the kind that so appealed to Elizabethan audiences. It mirrors Jessica's disguise as she escaped from Shylock's house and prepares for the crucial trial scene of Act 4, where Portia's intervention will radically affect the lives of every major male character.

The contrast in Act 3 that perhaps has received most critical attention concerns Shylock. He burns with resentment, anger and the desire to revenge. But Shakespeare gives him one of the best-known speeches in all his plays: his impassioned appeal to the common humanity of all peoples: 'Hath not a Jew eyes?' The speech may end with a justification of revenge, but its simplicity, power and eloquence has led to its being taken from its context and used as a universal statement for tolerance and respect.

# Act 4 Scene 1

Many productions open Scene 1, the 'trial scene', with a grand ceremonial entry of the Duke and the nobility of Venice. Historically, the Duke of Venice had not presided over a trial for over 200 years before Shakespeare's time, but his presence on stage brings obvious dramatic advantages. Trials in Venice were usually conducted with up to 40 judges drawn from the nobility and great traders (the Magnificoes) of the city.

It is probable that on Shakespeare's stage the Duke would sit near the back of the stage on a kind of throne with his fellow judges ranged either side of him. Antonio and his friends would be grouped on the right, the side traditionally associated with good. Shylock would enter from the left, the side associated with evil. The atmosphere in the early part of the scene is so intense that it seems as though Shylock himself is being tried, rather than having his case against Antonio heard. Shakespeare allows the allegedly fair and unbiased Duke of Venice to show partiality towards Antonio ('I am sorry for thee') and to express conventional Christian hostility towards Shylock:

> A stony adversary, an inhuman wretch,
> Uncapable of pity, void and empty
> From any dram of mercy.                     *(lines 4–6)*

Not for the first time in the play, Shylock is dehumanised and stripped of any humanitarian feelings of compassion and mercy. In striking contrast, Shakespeare gives Antonio a speech of great dignity and restraint. It seems designed to further heighten audience sympathy for Antonio and turn them against Shylock:

> I do oppose
> My patience to his fury, and am armed
> To suffer with a quietness of spirit
> The very tyranny and rage of his.           *(lines 10–13)*

The simple stage direction 'Enter Shylock' is often used to create a moment of great dramatic intensity. Many productions use it to underline the clash of the two religious factions of the play, and to show Shylock's position as an alien outsider. He remains silent as the Duke appeals to him, first using his name rather than the offensive

'Jew'. The Duke says that everyone believes Shylock is using brinkmanship, keeping up his pretence until the last possible moment, but will finally show mercy and remorse, and drop his suit against Antonio. The Duke encourages Shylock not only to cancel the forfeit of the pound of flesh but also, 'touched with human gentleness and love', to write off part of the original loan in view of Antonio's recent financial losses, which make even the hardest of hearts feel sorry for him. But significantly, the Duke ends with a line that can be spoken as a barely concealed threat:

> We all expect a gentle answer, Jew. *(line 34)*

Shylock's response is uncompromising. He has sworn a religious oath to pursue his bond, and he asserts that if the bond is denied it will imperil Venice's reputation as a place of law and freedom. Shylock refuses to give any explanation for his desire to have Antonio's flesh rather than 3,000 ducats. He merely asserts it is his 'humour': simply because he chooses. He offers a list of what other men find loathsome: 'a rat', 'a gaping pig', 'a cat', the noise of bagpipes. Such revulsions cannot be explained, he claims, and concludes

> So can I give no reason, nor I will not,
> More than a lodged hate and a certain loathing
> I bear Antonio. *(lines 59–61)*

Bassanio angrily declares that this is no answer to excuse Shylock's cruelty. Shylock retorts he is not compelled to please Bassanio with his answer, and the two men fence verbally over whether hated things or persons should be killed. Antonio, silent until now, intercedes, telling Bassanio of the futility of trying to reason with the pitiless Shylock. He compares the task of trying to change the Jew's mind to trying to hold back the tide, or prevent the wolf from eating the lamb, or stop the treetops moaning when blown by the wind. Antonio believes it impossible to soften Shylock's 'Jewish heart', and asks for quick judgement.

Bassanio offers twice the value of the bond, but Shylock refuses: 'I would have my bond.' He fears no retribution from the court, because he has done no wrong. In a challenging indictment of the social structure of Venice, Shylock argues that just as the Christians have bought slaves and treat them oppressively, so Shylock has bought the right to his pound of flesh and will not be denied. The laws of Venice must endorse his judgement or they are worthless:

> The pound of flesh which I demand of him
> Is dearly bought; 'tis mine, and I will have it.
> If you deny me, fie upon your law:
> There is no force in the decrees of Venice.　　　*(lines 99–102)*

Bassanio tries to rally Antonio's spirits, offering himself as sacrifice, but Antonio is stoically resigned to death, describing himself as a 'tainted wether of the flock', a sick ram, suited to be killed. As Nerissa, disguised as a lawyer's clerk, brings news from Bellario in Padua, Shylock dominates the stage, sharpening his knife on the sole of his shoe. His action enrages Gratiano, who accuses him bitterly:

> O be thou damned, inexecrable dog,
> And for thy life let justice be accused!
>
> . . .
>
> 　　　　　　　for thy desires
> Are wolfish, bloody, starved, and ravenous.　　　*(lines 128–38)*

But Shylock has the upper hand. He mocks Gratiano, saying his words may be loud and angry, but they are empty abuse, making no difference to the terms of the bond or the law. The 'seal' on the bond is impossible to remove, and Shylock sums up his position in the simplest but most effective words: 'I stand here for law.' His words dramatically precede news of the defence lawyer. Bellario's letter tells that Balthazar (the disguised Portia) will stand in for him to defend Antonio. Bellario's glowing testimony sets the stage for Portia's entrance. Her disguise, according to dramatic convention, is impenetrable. Even her husband does not recognise her. Only Nerissa and the audience know her true identity.

Portia's first four words. 'I did, my lord', all monosyllables, suggest she will be purposeful and direct. That impression is confirmed as she takes charge of the proceedings. Portia's clipped, efficient style hints at the dramatic conflict to come. Her questioning of Shylock is often played as highly formal and businesslike, but her opening question can often evoke audience laughter because the answer is usually glaringly obvious to all:

> Which is the merchant here and which the Jew?     *(line 170)*

Portia's question may be a scornful dismissal of Shylock's presence, intended to discomfort him as another attack on his identity. But occasionally the question is justified. For example, in one Royal Shakespeare Company production, which was staged in modern dress, Shylock was played as a fully assimilated Jew. His smart city suit and his entire appearance were identical to that of the Christians.

Portia declares that Shylock's case is 'of a strange nature', but that there is nothing within the law of Venice to prevent him from proceeding. Her command that Shylock must be merciful, and his prickly response ('On what compulsion must I?') evokes the speech which has become world-famous as a poetic expression of the attributes of mercy:

> The quality of mercy is not strained,
> It droppeth as the gentle rain from heaven
> Upon the place beneath. It is twice blest:
> It blesseth him that gives, and him that takes.
> 'Tis mightiest in the mightiest, it becomes
> The thronèd monarch better than his crown.
> His sceptre shows the force of temporal power,
> The attribute to awe and majesty,
> Wherein doth sit the dread and fear of kings;
> But mercy is above this sceptred sway.
> It is enthronèd in the hearts of kings,
> It is an attribute to God himself,
> And earthly power doth then show likest God's
> When mercy seasons justice.     *(lines 180–93)*

Portia's speech counterbalances Shylock's desire for revenge. In Act 3 Scene 1 Shylock had declared his common humanity with all other men: 'Hath not a Jew eyes?' Now Shakespeare expresses why mercy is such a necessary virtue of humanity. It is as free and bountiful as 'gentle rain', bestowing grace on the giver and the receiver. It is the supreme quality that any king can possess, greater than any earthly authority he commands, because mercy is divine. It is a quality of God Himself. When monarchs exercise mercy in their justice, their power seems most like God's own power.

Her speech is eloquent and moving, but it is also a resolute confrontation of Shylock's hard-heartedness. She draws her conclusion, addressing him directly (and perhaps offensively) as 'Jew'. He demands justice, but justice alone will not allow access to heaven. Only mercy can. Just as we pray for mercy, we should ourselves behave mercifully. But Shylock is deaf to Portia's argument. He may also feel offended, seeing an annoying pun in 'gentle' (Gentile), and finding a condescending echo of the Christian Lord's Prayer ('forgive us our trespasses') in her reminder 'We do pray for mercy'. His response is unequivocal:

> My deeds upon my head! I crave the law,
> The penalty and forfeit of my bond.                  *(lines 202–3)*

Bassanio offers Shylock 6,000 ducats to clear the bond, declaring that if that is insufficient he will pay ten times more, 'On forfeit of my hands, my head, my heart.' If Shylock does not accept then Bassanio can only acknowledge that hatred triumphs over honesty. He begs Portia (failing to recognise he is speaking to his wife) to use all her ingenuity to twist the law. His line stands as almost a classic statement that the end justifies the means:

> To do a great right, do a little wrong                  *(line 212)*

Portia seems to offer no hope. No power in Venice can change the law. To do so would set a dangerous precedent, certain to lead to a flood of dubious legal challenges. Shylock is exultant. He praises Portia's wisdom, honouring her as 'a Daniel' (a Jewish prophet renowned for catching out liars), and as 'most reverend doctor'. He rejects the offer of three times the value of the debt, and adamantly insists upon the unbreakability of the contract, the bond that Portia now scrutinises:

> An oath, an oath. I have an oath in heaven!
> Shall I lay perjury upon my soul?
> No, not for Venice.                  *(lines 224–6)*

Portia declares the bond legal. It must be honoured, and Shylock is entitled to cut a pound of flesh from near Antonio's heart. Portia again urges 'Be merciful', and offers to tear up the bond on Shylock's order. But Shylock is adamant. The bond can only be destroyed when the forfeit has been paid 'according to the tenour': its precise terms. Shylock's insistence on the small print, the letter of the law, will shortly rebound disastrously upon him. But at the moment, with Portia playing what will prove to be a cat-and-mouse game with him, dramatic tension mounts as it seems Shylock really will be able to exact his bloody revenge on Antonio. Portia tells Antonio her chilling judgement, and Shylock gives his ecstatic response:

PORTIA   You must prepare your bosom for his knife.
SHYLOCK   O noble judge, O excellent young man!     *(lines 241–2)*

Portia and Shylock go on to share lines, a dramatic device which conventionally increases pace and so heightens excitement. Shylock savours the exact words on the bond which allow him to cut 'Nearest his heart', but Portia seems concerned with legal niceties. She asks if scales are at hand to weigh the flesh. Shylock instantly confirms they are, but replies in a different tone to Portia's request that he have a surgeon present to staunch the flow of blood. Again, his insistence on the exact terms of his contract, and no more, will prove his downfall:

Is it so nominated in the bond?     *(line 255)*

On stage, Shylock often mockingly scrutinises the bond with great intensity as he declares he can find nothing in it about a surgeon. Portia invites Antonio to speak, but, perhaps in a show of complete impartiality, addresses him not by name but as 'merchant'. Antonio declares he is prepared for death. He takes Bassanio's hand, asking him not to grieve, but to tell Portia of Antonio's love for him. That deep affection is evident in his farewell, but so too is the dramatic irony in Antonio's 'Commend me to your honourable wife.' Portia listens silently as Antonio professes his love for Bassanio.

Bassanio's reply reveals his own powerful feelings for his friend as he vows he would give everything, including his wife, if he could deliver Antonio from the 'devil', Shylock. Portia comments tartly on his pledge:

Your wife would give you little thanks for that
If she were by to hear you make the offer.          *(lines 284–5)*

Nerissa makes a similarly acerbic comment as Gratiano wishes he
could exchange his wife's life for Shylock's change of mind. The two
women's remarks on their husbands provide a brief comic interlude
in the tense courtroom atmosphere, but Shakespeare returns Shylock
to the centre of attention. He dismisses all Christian husbands and
wishes his daughter had married even the most vile of Jews, rather
than a Christian. He demands his bond, and Portia confirms the court
must award it. Shylock's words to Antonio express his murderous
intent: 'come, prepare.'

All productions attempt to make the moment almost unbearable to
watch, as Antonio stands, his bare chest exposed, with Shylock's knife
poised over his heart. The actors want the audience to feel they really
are about to witness a bloody action. They strive to create a long
moment of heart-stopping intensity before Portia speaks her words
which relieve the agonising suspense:

Tarry a little, there is something else.          *(line 301)*

Shylock is confounded as Portia insists on the letter of the bond.
Shylock may take his pound of flesh, but no blood. Justice must be
absolute and precise. If he takes the tiniest amount more or less than
a pound he will be executed and all his wealth confiscated by the
Venetian state. Gratiano seizes the opportunity to mockingly imitate
all Shylock's previous praise of Portia. His racism is all too evident,
and he echoes each phrase with relish:

O Jew, an upright judge, a learned judge!          *(line 319)*
A Daniel, still say I, a second Daniel!          *(line 336)*

Shylock knows he is trapped by his own insistence on the precise
terms of the bond. Portia refuses him the previously-offered threefold
repayment, then the principal itself. He may have nothing but his
bond. Shylock wishes to leave, but Portia delivers another judgement.
Because he has broken the law of Venice by making an attempt on
the life of one of its citizens, all Shylock's wealth must be confiscated,
half going to Antonio, half to the state. His own life now lies at the

mercy of the Duke. Gratiano derisively orders him to beg for mercy, but before Shylock can speak, the Duke pardons him, sparing his life.

Antonio seems to show similar mercy, asking that Shylock retain half his goods. That half he must eventually leave to Lorenzo and Jessica. The other half is to be held in trust by Antonio, and will also go, on Shylock's death, to Lorenzo. These financial conditions seem to have some regard for Shylock, but Antonio's further condition must surely be deeply offensive to Shylock, as it is to any Jew, in any age. He must become a Christian. Harold Bloom (see pages 92–3) finds it utterly improbable that Shylock could possibly agree ('I am content') to conversion. In some productions the line has been cut, not just because of its effect on Shylock, but because it shows the Christian Antonio as cruelly vindictive, striking at the heart of Shylock's deepest religious convictions.

On stage, each actor playing Shylock must decide how he should leave the court as he speaks his final low-key, monosyllabic lines. Sometimes he leaves with great dignity, ignoring Gratiano's taunting abuse. Sometimes he exits as a broken and humiliated man, his suffering all too evident. Laurence Olivier made his exit with quiet self-assurance, but after he was out of sight he uttered a long scream of anguish that expressed his feelings of total loss.

The final episode of the scene develops the 'rings' plot. Bassanio thanks Portia for saving the life of his friend and offers any gift she chooses. She asks for his gloves, then for his ring. Bassanio refuses to part with the ring, explaining it was given to him by his wife. Portia mocks his refusal, but leaves, presumably pleased that he holds her gift so dear:

PORTIA   Give me your gloves, I'll wear them for your sake;
        And for your love I'll take this ring from you.
        Do not draw back your hand; I'll take no more,
        And you in love shall not deny me this.
BASSANIO   This ring, good sir? Alas, it is a trifle;
        I will not shame myself to give you this.
PORTIA   I will have nothing else but only this;
        And now methinks I have a mind to it.
BASSANIO   There's more depends on this than on the value.
        The dearest ring in Venice will I give you,

> And find it out by proclamation.
> Only for this I pray you pardon me.
> PORTIA    I see, sir, you are liberal in offers.
> You taught me first to beg, and now methinks
> You teach me how a beggar should be answered.
> BASSANIO    Good sir, this ring was given me by my wife,
> And when she put it on, she made me vow
> That I should neither sell, nor give, nor lose it.
> PORTIA    That scuse serves many men to save their gifts;
> And if your wife be not a mad woman,
> And know how well I have deserved this ring,
> She would not hold out enemy for ever
> For giving it to me. Well, peace be with you.    *(lines 422–44)*

But Shakespeare has comic business ahead in mind, so Antonio urges Bassanio to hand over the ring. Bassanio immediately sends Gratiano to give the ring to the disguised Portia. His action not only prepares for the comic consequences that will follow, but also signifies the strength of his feeling for Antonio. His friend's wish has more power than the vow he made to his wife.

## Act 4 Scene 2

This brief scene adds a further twist to the 'rings' plot. Gratiano catches up with the disguised women and hands over Bassanio's ring to Portia. She is first taken aback by Bassanio's betrayal of his promise: 'That cannot be.' But, recovering her composure, she asks Gratiano to show Nerissa the way to Shylock's house to deliver the deed of agreement. Nerissa plans to make Gratiano hand over his ring too, and Portia's lines predict the comedy that will come in Act 5 as the two women force humiliating confessions from their husbands:

> We shall have old swearing
> That they did give the rings away to men;
> But we'll outface them, and outswear them too.    *(lines 15–17)*

## Act 4: Critical review

The long trial scene which occupies virtually all of Act 4 has often been judged to be the heart of the play. It is the best-known episode in *The Merchant of Venice*, and the climactic turning point of the drama. The tables are turned on Shylock, his thirst for revenge is confounded, and he is utterly humiliated. Act 4 grippingly builds suspense, with victory snatched only at the very last moment.

Critics typically argue that the act displays most clearly the theme of the struggle between justice and mercy. Portia's moving declaration in her speech that begins 'The quality of mercy is not strained' summarises the argument that justice is most appropriately done when mercy tempers it.

Although the act reveals yet again the bitter division between Christian and Jew, Portia appeals to religious principles common to both faiths. Both assert the divine sanction of mercy. Her speech would have touched a familiar chord with certain members of Shakespeare's audience, because the conflicting claims of justice and mercy was a common debating topic in schools and among lawyers.

But the act shows that debate is one thing, and action another. What follows Portia's speech demonstrates the difficulty of achieving that humane balance between justice and mercy for which she pleads. Shylock denies mercy, insisting on the precise terms of his bond. It stipulates no surgeon to save Antonio's life, so no merciful help is to be given. But his insistence on the letter of the law rebounds disastrously on him, and although Shylock's life is spared, he receives little other mercy from the Christians. Most punishing is the demand that he become a Christian: a sentence that is the equivalent of spiritual death.

Gratiano's sneering mockery shows all too clearly the ugly face of anti-Semitism. Shakespeare raises troubling questions about whether Shylock deserves the treatment he eventually receives. But he also portrays him in a totally negative light as, for instance, when he so deliberately whets his knife to cut Antonio's flesh.

With the revenge plot ended, Shakespeare has comedy in mind. The husbands hand over their rings, and so prepare for Act 5 when the women will outwit and humble the men.

# Act 5 Scene 1

Once again Shakespeare juxtaposes settings as Act 5 returns to Belmont. The high drama of the trial scene gives way to a seemingly relaxed world of romance. The intensity of Shylock's hatred, his insistence on his bond, his humiliating defeat and Gratiano's grating racism are in sharpest contrast with the tranquil mood of this scene's opening. Shakespeare turns from near-tragedy and animosity to comedy and love.

Lorenzo and Jessica appear to be a typically romantic couple whose dramatic purpose is to express the harmony of love. The phrase 'In such a night', repeated eight times, is more than a reminder to the audience of the time. It suffuses their dialogue with a dreamlike, ritualistic quality. Its patterned repetition confirms the artifice of the lovers' exchange. Their shared lines and balanced phrases suggest perfect harmony. Shakespeare is working within the tradition of romance, and writes an episode in striking contrast with the harrowing disputes of the previous act.

Lorenzo sets the scene: a bright moon, the sweet wind kissing the trees. The setting is perfect. He and Jessica recall the deeds of famous legendary lovers on similar fairy-tale nights. Shakespeare knew the stories from his reading of Chaucer and Ovid (see pages 62–4) and his style here has the same mythical, fanciful qualities. On the surface, the stories are of love, but all have sombre echoes of tragedy, betrayal and loss. All reflect aspects of what has happened in *The Merchant of Venice*:

- Troilus climbed the walls of Troy to be with his lover Cressida. She later betrayed him.
- Thisbe met her lover Pyramus secretly and against her father's wishes. Their love pact ended in suicide.
- Dido, Queen of Carthage, spent a night like this on the shore trying to entice her lover, Aeneas, back to her. But he had deserted her.
- Medea gathered enchanted herbs to refresh Aeson, the father of her lover Jason, whom she had helped to win the Golden Fleece. She was later deserted by him.

Lorenzo incorporates Jessica's own experience into the list of lovers. Punning on 'steal', he tells how she deserted her father, stole his money and eloped with Lorenzo:

> In such a night
> Did Jessica steal from the wealthy Jew
> And with an unthrift love did run from Venice
> As far as Belmont.                                        *(lines 14–17)*

Jessica's response mirrors the rhythms and phrasing of Lorenzo's lines. She seems to tease her husband that his vows of love are not true. Lorenzo uses a similar style to deny her claim. The exchange has been played on stage both as playful banter and as edgy needling which does not augur well for their relationship. It is ended by the arrival of Stephano, who announces Portia's imminent return, and tells that she has visited certain holy places, praying that her marriage will be blessed. Whether Stephano's report is true, or whether it is yet another of Portia's fictions is unclear. But his claim that she has adopted a 'holy hermit' as a companion casts doubt on Stephano's tale: the 'holy hermit' never appears.

Lancelot's entrance provides a brief comic interlude. In the darkness he finds it difficult to see Lorenzo and so uses hunting cries to locate him: 'Sola, sola!' Lancelot excitedly tells that Bassanio will shortly arrive. His news prompts Lorenzo to order music to welcome Portia and Bassanio. His speech to Jessica, extolling the virtues of music, has become one of the most famous examples of Shakespeare's lyrical verse, praised equally for its melodiousness and its subject matter:

> How sweet the moonlight sleeps upon this bank!
> Here will we sit, and let the sounds of music
> Creep in our ears; soft stillness and the night
> Become the touches of sweet harmony.
> Sit, Jessica. Look how the floor of heaven
> Is thick inlaid with patens of bright gold.
> There's not the smallest orb which thou behold'st
> But in his motion like an angel sings,
> Still choiring to the young-eyed cherubins.
> Such harmony is in immortal souls,
> But whilst this muddy vesture of decay
> Doth grossly close it in, we cannot hear it.        *(lines 54–65)*

Lorenzo describes the ancient belief in 'the music of the spheres'.

That belief stretches back at least to the time of Plato in the fourth century BC. It held that the moving stars and planets revolved on crystal spheres, and made heavenly music as they orbited. Once again, as at the scene's opening, the mood is dreamlike, mythical, romantic. Lorenzo's sensual language uses religious imagery. The sky is described as 'the floor of heaven'. It is 'inlaid with patens' (the stars are compared to plates used at Holy Communion), and inhabited by angels and 'young-eyed cherubins'. But men and women whose 'immortal souls' are enclosed by merely human bodies ('this muddy vesture of decay') cannot hear the harmony. Lorenzo's conclusion is a sombre reminder of the imperfections of humanity.

Lorenzo's conclusion may be the reason why Jessica declares that music does not cheer her. But her husband seems to rebuke her, saying that her sad mood comes from being so sensitive to music's effects. He claims that wild animals are entranced by soothing music, and describes how Orpheus, a legendary Greek, used music to charm trees, stones and floods. He asserts that music has healing powers, and that any man who does not respond to it must be villainous and untrustworthy: 'fit for treasons, stratagems, and spoils'. His words may be an unconscious criticism of Shylock, who in Act 2 Scene 5 dismissed the music of Christian masques as 'shallow foppery'.

As Lorenzo and Jessica listen to the musicians, they do not notice the return of Portia and Nerissa. Traditionally, critics note that Portia's first lines echo a similar expression in the Gospel of St Matthew in the Bible. Some go on to claim the lines symbolise Portia's association with light, and refer to the service she has just performed in saving Antonio's life:

> That light we see is burning in my hall.
> How far that little candle throws his beams!
> So shines a good deed in a naughty world.          *(lines 89–91)*

Nerissa points out, perhaps ironically, that the candle was unnoticed when the moon shone. Her remark prompts Portia to reflect on relative values. A substitute king will appear regal until compared to a true king. An inland river is nothing compared to the sea. Only by comparison can the true worth of anything be established and appreciated. How Portia's reflections relate to the play has been very differently interpreted. For example, she may be thinking of herself either humbly (a 'brook') or immodestly ('the main of waters' – the sea), or she may be comparing Lorenzo ('A substitute') with herself ('a king').

Portia continues her comparisons as the two women listen to the music. She claims that music sounds better at night than during the day but acknowledges that all judgements of value arise from human perception and thought: 'Nothing is good, I see, without respect'. Her comparison of the song of the crow and the lark illustrates her claim. Only when they are heard by humans can judgement of quality be made. Portia goes on to claim that time and place affect such judgements. Everything has its appropriate season. Her thoughts on value here presage a similar reflection Shakespeare would put in the mouth of Hamlet a few years later:

> For there is nothing either good or bad, but thinking makes
> it so.                    *(Hamlet Act 2 Scene 2, lines 239–40)*

In the theatre there is often a long, tranquil pause in the action as Portia and the others listen to the harmony of the music. At last Lorenzo becomes aware of Portia and welcomes her home. Portia orders that Bassanio and Gratiano, shortly to arrive, must not be told that she and Jessica left Belmont.

Some editors choose to divide Act 5 into two scenes, beginning the second scene here as dawn breaks and the husbands enter. This final episode will mainly be the humorous dénouement of the 'rings' plot. Portia immediately begins to tease Bassanio: 'Let me give light, but let me not be light'. She will provide light to guide him, but will not be provocative or unfaithful (a common Elizabethan meaning of 'light'). She puns on her husband's description of Antonio as the man 'To whom I am so infinitely bound':

> You should in all sense be much bound to him,
> For as I hear he was much bound for you.          *(lines 136–7)*

Her wordplay has comic, serious and barbed possibilities. The repetition may be humorous, but 'bound' also signifies Antonio's imprisonment and Bassanio's financial debt to him. Perhaps Portia is hinting she feels ambivalent about Bassanio having borrowed money to woo her.

Antonio's welcome to Belmont seems much warmer than that received by Jessica in Act 3, but as Portia greets him, a quarrel breaks out between Gratiano and Nerissa. She accuses him that despite all his vows he has given his ring to 'a judge's clerk'. The comedy of the 'rings' plot moves into top gear as Nerissa piles on her accusations, Gratiano attempts to wriggle out of his difficulty, and Portia, with mock solemnity, mischievously stirs the pot and inflames the dispute. She rebukes Gratiano and declares she is confident her own husband would never do such a thing as part with the ring she gave him. Bassanio squirms in silent embarrassment, knowing he will shortly be called to account. He declares his discomfort in a comic aside:

> Why, I were best to cut my left hand off
> And swear I lost the ring defending it.           *(lines 177–8)*

Within the comedy, Shakespeare reinforces thematic concerns of the play. Nerissa seizes on the issue of value. She declares the intrinsic worth of the ring is not significant. What matters is the love pledge it betokens. In her mock-angry, humorous comparison, the value systems of Venice and Belmont – money versus love – are thrown into relief. And Nerissa's remark that 'The clerk will ne'er wear hair on's face that had it' is an obvious reminder of the trial and of disguise. It implies that Gratiano has been lying and has given up his ring to a woman. Which, of course, he has!

Both husbands suffer comically at the hands of their wives, who feign surprise and anger. Bassanio now faces his inevitable moment of accountability. He too is forced to admit he has handed over his wife's ring. The two women very obviously win the battle of the sexes. Portia caps the victory by declaring that Bassanio is banned from her bed until the ring is regained, and both women threaten to be unfaithful with the men to whom their rings have been given. The whole episode is usually deliciously funny on stage, the humour obviously benign and playfully teasing. But it has occasionally been played with a degree of spite or cruelty underlying the tormenting of the husbands (to which they have responded with resentment).

Certainly the episode has uncanny echoes of the trial scene. Portia once again traps a male by exploiting the man's inability to fulfil the terms of a bond. She mocks the oath of faithfulness that Bassanio now swears, but this time, in contrast to what happened at the trial, it is

Antonio who speaks up for Bassanio. He apologises that he is once again the unfortunate cause of the quarrel, but swears that his friend will always keep faith in the future. This time he pledges his soul as collateral. Once again Antonio is 'bound'.

Portia at last relents. She gives Bassanio a new ring as a love pledge (which of course is the original one). Bassanio's surprise at seeing it is another delightful comic moment but it is undercut again by Portia's revelation that she gained it from the lawyer in return for sleeping with him. Gratiano is informed that he too has been made a cuckold (a man with an unfaithful wife).

In the dénouement Shakespeare unravels the complex plots. Portia's brusque and efficient explanation of the disguises, and her report that Antonio's trading ships have come safely and profitably home renders him speechless: 'I am dumb.' As Bassanio and Gratiano consider the prospect of at last bedding their wives and Antonio savours the news of his ships, Nerissa hands to Lorenzo and Jessica the deed of gift produced by Shylock. When he dies, all his wealth comes to his daughter and son-in-law. Yet again Shylock is unnamed, referred to only as the 'rich Jew'. The play is often thought of as his, but he has been absent throughout the fifth act. To Lorenzo, the news of his fortune is like heavenly food ('manna') to starving people.

Portia affirms that it is almost morning. She promises a full explanation of all that has happened, and uses the language of the courtroom:

> . . . charge us there upon inter'gatories,
> And we will answer all things faithfully. *(lines 298–9)*

Gratiano concludes the play. In rhyming couplets he muses on whether Nerissa wants to go to bed now or wait until the following night. He looks forward to 'couching with the doctor's clerk', and his final word, the last word in the play, is 'ring'. It is an obvious reminder of the sexual meaning of the word for Elizabethans (female genitals), and a reminder of the need to protect and value love tokens:

> Well, while I live I'll fear no other thing
> So sore as keeping safe Nerissa's ring. *(lines 306–7)*

Some productions are not satisfied with ending the play on a light-hearted comic note. In one staging, the lights faded on the sight of Shylock at prayer. In another, Jessica was left alone and desolate as all the Christians went off, ignoring her. Because every play is an invitation to directors and actors to use their imagination, such stagings, although not specified in the text, are legitimate and moving reminders of the central preoccupations of *The Merchant of Venice*.

## Act 5: Critical review

Some critics have argued that the play would retain its dramatic integrity if it ended with the conclusion of the trial scene in Act 4, with Shylock defeated and Antonio saved. But it is evident that Shakespeare is concerned to continue to explore, in the lyrical and comic episodes of Act 5, the themes that had preoccupied the drama of the first four acts.

The themes of reality and appearance, and of justice and mercy, receive light-hearted treatment in this act. The discomforting of Bassanio and Gratiano is achieved by their failure to recognise their own wives. They had earlier handed over their rings to the disguised Portia and Nerissa; now they pay the penalty for their inability to see beyond outward appearance. But the 'justice' meted out to them is tempered with 'mercy' in comic vein. They suffer only embarrassment, and perhaps learn from their short-sightedness.

After the atmosphere of rancorous hatred in Act 4, the theme of love returns renewed in Act 5. It takes very different expressions. The rapturous verse of Lorenzo and Jessica contrasts with the teasing to which Portia and Nerissa subject their husbands. The first style comes from an older world of idealised romance, where music and stars have seemingly supernatural significance. The second seems much more modern in its edgy, rather barbed tone. For Portia and Nerissa love now seems more conditional, less total and undemanding.

Male friendship too seems qualified. Antonio once again declares his commitment to Bassanio, but at the play's end he seems an isolated figure. His financial fortunes have been restored, his life has been saved, but the person he holds most dear is now married to the woman who prevented Shylock from taking revenge on him.

And what of Shylock? He does not appear in Act 5. There is only news that he has willed his remaining wealth to Jessica and Lorenzo. Although Act 5 has traditionally been interpreted and staged as unequivocally suggesting concord and reconciliation, more recent interpretations argue that the sour, antagonistic atmosphere of the first four acts make it impossible to erase its unpleasant bitterness from the seeming harmony of Act 5. This is reflected in the staging of the final scene.

## Contexts

The hugely enjoyable film *Shakespeare in Love* portrays a popular belief about the source of Shakespeare's creativity. It shows him suffering from 'writer's block', unable to put pen to paper, with no idea of how to write his next play. But all is resolved when he meets a beautiful young girl. His love for her sparks an overwhelming flow of creative energy – and he writes *Romeo and Juliet*!

It is an attractive idea, and the film presents it delightfully, but the truth of the matter is far more complex. Like every other writer, Shakespeare was influenced by many factors other than his own personal experience. The society of his time, its practices, beliefs and language in political and economic affairs, culture and religion, were the raw materials on which his imagination worked.

This section first identifies the three texts from which all later editions of *The Merchant of Venice* derive. It then discusses the contexts from which *The Merchant of Venice* emerged: the wide range of different influences which fostered the creativity of Shakespeare as he wrote the play. These contexts ensured that *The Merchant of Venice* is full of all kinds of reminders of everyday life, and the familiar knowledge, assumptions, beliefs and values of Elizabethan England.

## What did Shakespeare write?

Sometime around 1596–7, William Shakespeare, already known as a successful playwright, wrote *The Merchant of Venice*. It was probably first performed in 1597. What was the play that Shakespeare wrote and his audiences heard? No one knows for certain because his original script has not survived, nor have any handwritten amendments he might subsequently have made. So what is the origin of the text of the play you are studying? Most scholars today agree with the following account of how the text of today's editions was established.

The first published version of the play appeared in 1600, and is known as the First Quarto (a quarto page is about the same size as this page you are reading). Its title page described it as 'The comicall History of the Merchant of Venice' and boasted that it was already popular on stage, having been 'divers [many] times acted by the Lord Chamberlaine his servants' – Shakespeare's own company. Most scholars believe that the First Quarto was probably compiled from Shakespeare's manuscript and is therefore generally regarded as reliable.

Shakespeare died in 1616. Another edition, the Second Quarto, was published in 1619 and in 1623 the First Folio, containing 36 plays, was published (a folio page is around two times larger than this page). Both later editions follow the First Quarto closely, making only slight changes such as adding directions for musical effects and adjusting the text to avoid profane exclamations and critical references to the Scots, which was important, as King James was now on the throne. (The word 'Scottish' was discreetly changed to 'other' when used in a negative context.) One of the minor confusions occurring between the different editions centres on the variants of the names Salarino, Solanio and Salerio and whether Shakespeare intended to establish two or three separate characters.

Ever since the play's first publication, editors have made a multitude of judgements in adjusting the play as they have looked at the various versions in use during or shortly after Shakespeare's lifetime. This guide follows the New Cambridge edition of the play (also used in Cambridge School Shakespeare).

# What did Shakespeare read?

Shakespeare's genius lay in his ability to transform what he read into gripping drama. This section is therefore about the influence of genre: the literary contexts of *The Merchant of Venice* in both elite and popular culture. It identifies the stories and dramatic conventions that fired Shakespeare's imagination as he wrote the play.

*The Merchant of Venice* is a skilful blending of three different stories. First, there is the tale of the 'bond' involving the pound of flesh. Second, there is the casket story. Finally, there is the elopement of the daughter with her lover. All three stories were well known long before Shakespeare gave them dramatic life, as they existed throughout Europe in numerous folk tales and myths. Shakespeare would have known such tales. They were part of the popular culture of his time, and they would have been in his mind as he wrote the play.

## The story of Gianetto and the courtship of the Lady

Although no one can be certain of the exact source, many scholars agree that Shakespeare based the play on a contemporary Italian short story, the tale of Gianetto of Venice and the Lady of Belmont. He found it in a collection of stories called *Il Pecorone*, which best translates into English as 'The Idiot' or 'The Simpleton'. The tales were written by Ser Giovanni of Florence and published in Italy in 1558.

Ansaldo is a wealthy Venetian merchant who supplies a lavishly-provisioned ship to his godson Gianetto and encourages him to sail out in search of further trade and profit. Gianetto lands in Belmont and meets a rich Lady who lives there. He learns that she will offer her hand in marriage only to the man who is able to spend the night and have sex with her. Any man who agrees to this 'test' and fails will forfeit all of his belongings to her. The Lady ensures that she never loses by giving all of her suitors drugged wine. By this method she deviously protects her virtue and ensures that she regularly tricks her suitors out of their possessions. Gianetto is not clever enough to spot the trick and he consequently loses his ship, returning to Venice in embarrassment.

Gianetto lies to Ansaldo that his first ship has been lost at sea and he is duly provided with a second vessel by his understanding godfather. Once again, Gianetto loses this ship to the Lady and Ansaldo can only consider funding a third voyage if he borrows heavily to finance Gianetto's expedition. He therefore agrees to pledge a pound of his own flesh to a wealthy Jew, who lends him 10,000 ducats. When Gianetto attempts the 'test' for the third time he is warned about the drugged wine by the Lady's maid and he thus wins the hand of the Lady and quickly assumes the position of Lord of Belmont.

Gianetto forgets all about the bond he has struck with the Jew until the day of reckoning arrives. The Lady of Belmont responds to news of Ansaldo's plight by sending Gianetto back to Venice with 100,000 ducats to pay off the bond. The Jew, however, will not be bought so easily and insists on pursuing his case to judgement.

The Lady arrives in Venice, disguised as a lawyer, and tries to persuade the Jew to take the 100,000 ducats, only to be denied. When the case goes to court she informs the Jew of the conditions of the forfeit, namely that the flesh taken must weigh exactly one pound and that no blood can be spilt. The penalty is the Jew's life. When he cannot even recoup the original capital of the loan, the Jew tears up the bond in a furious rage.

Gianetto wants to pay the lawyer but the lawyer insists on having Gianetto's ring, which was a love-gift from his Lady. Gianetto takes Ansaldo with him when he returns to Belmont, where he is met with a frosty reception. The Lady forces home her advantage and torments Gianetto mercilessly until she finally discloses that she was, in fact, the lawyer who received the ring. All is harmoniously resolved when Ansaldo is paired off with the Lady's maid who helped Gianetto during the love test.

Such a stark outline does scant justice to the intricacies of the original tale. But it is clear how closely Shakespeare followed the model and, also, what changes he made as he adapted the story into *The Merchant of Venice*:

- The bond of the pound of flesh appears in both versions.
- The device of the rings follows broadly similar lines, but Shakespeare turns it into a more obviously comic device by adding the parallel story of Gratiano and Nerissa.
- The climax of the trial scene is almost duplicated. The Lady takes the Jew to the brink of his anticipated victory, even allowing the Jew to unsheath his knife. She dramatically halts proceedings and saves Ansaldo by the legal loophole.
- Ansaldo's selfless forbearance and indulgence of his unattractive godson's quest echoes strongly the relationship between Antonio and Bassanio. Shakespeare seems to have made the relationship between Antonio and Bassanio charged with homoerotic nuances.
- The Jew in the story, like Shylock, was spurred on by both religious and mercantile considerations in pursuit of his judgement against the debtor.
- The final marriage between Ansaldo and the woman was cut from *The Merchant of Venice*. That marriage was replaced by Gratiano's wedding to Nerissa in Act 3.
- Although it is clear how Gianetto has lost his fortune (seized by the Lady of Belmont), his equivalent in *The Merchant of Venice*, Bassanio, is penniless for a different reason. Bassanio has indulged in a standard of living he could not afford: 'By something showing a more swelling port / Than my faint means would grant continuance.'

## The *Gesta Romanorum*

Shakespeare also drew upon a medieval tale from a collection called the *Gesta Romanorum*, published in London in 1577. He found in it the idea of the caskets (gold, silver and lead) as the means of proving worthiness in marriage. This concept replaces the drugged wine and the Lady's 'test' in *Il Pecorone*. Shakespeare also allows Portia to receive three different suitors (Morocco, Arragon and Bassanio) rather than the same suitor three times.

The elopement of Jessica and Lorenzo probably came from yet another source. Shakespeare would have been familiar with the tale from a fifteenth-century Italian writer, Masuccio of Salerno. The basic ingredients of the story were fairly traditional and widely known. It tells of a beautiful heroine and her clever, attractive male partner who is in debt to her father. She uses the help of a servant to escape from her mean father to be with the young man. The story examines the generation gap, the contrast between the poor youngsters and the rich parent figure.

## *The Jew of Malta*

At the time when Shakespeare sat down to write *The Merchant of Venice* there was huge popular interest in the fate of one Jew in particular, the Queen's physician, Roderigo Lopez (see page 67). His notoriety (he was accused of trying to poison the Queen) sparked a revival in the performances of another topical play with a Jewish central character, Christopher Marlowe's *The Jew of Malta*. Since Marlowe's play was written between the years 1589 and 1590, it may well have been one with which Shakespeare was familiar, and it is possible to see how Shakespeare's own story was influenced by what he knew.

Although described on the title page of the 1633 edition as a tragedy, *The Jew of Malta* is more like a political farce or melodrama. Its first recorded performance was in 1592 at the Rose Theatre in Bankside, London.

It recounts how Farnese, the Christian governor of Malta, takes the wealth of Barabas, a rich Jew, in order to pay off the Turks, who are demanding their tribute. Farnese feels able to justify seizing the money as he explains that Malta is cursed for allowing Jews to live there. He gives Barabas the choice of becoming a Christian and keeping half of his wealth or remaining a Jew and losing it all.

Barabas, a man of principle and defiance, chooses to remain loyal to his faith. He promptly sets off in search of revenge against the hypocritical Maltese leaders by playing the Christians off against the Turks. From these potentially tragic openings the plot quickly degenerates into a series of farcical manoeuvres. Barabas, unlike Marlowe's other great tragic figures, becomes little more than a comic embodiment of seething and obsessive hatred. As Barabas' plotting and scheming becomes more acute, he finally perishes. The revenging Farnese double-crosses him and at the end of the play sends him through a trapdoor into a boiling cauldron.

Marlowe uses the play to explore the theme of Jew against Christian. He underlines the contrast between what men claim to believe and what they actually do. The Christians are hypocrites and Barabas detests them:

> Rather had I, a Jew, be hated thus,
> Than pitied in a Christian poverty.
> For I can see no fruits in all their faith
> But malice, falsehood, and excessive pride,
> Which methinks fits not their profession.

Like Shylock in *The Merchant of Venice*, Barabas has a daughter, Abigail, whom he loves more than anything except his gold. Barabas cries 'O girl, O gold, O beauty, O my bliss' and hugs his money bags and his daughter in turn. Later, Barabas poisons Abigail with a pot of porridge. Shakespeare perhaps had this in mind when he was writing these words for Shylock : 'O my ducats, O my daughter!' and 'would she were hearsed at my foot, and the ducats in her coffin.'

## Classical sources

*The Merchant of Venice* is also full of classical references. Books such as Ovid's *Metamorphoses* and Plutarch's *Lives* were among Shakespeare's favourite reading. He was also very familiar with the works of the Middle English poet, Geoffrey Chaucer. They furnished him with many stories and all kinds of references and images which he incorporated into his play:

- Bassanio's pursuit of Portia is likened to Jason's hazardous quest to retrieve the Golden Fleece from the shores of Colchis ('Colchos' strand') on the Black Sea. After Bassanio has passed the test of the caskets, Gratiano compares the two men's fate to that of the Argonauts (Jason's crew): 'We are the Jasons, we have won the fleece' (Act 3 Scene 2, line 240).

- Portia pledges not to break the conditions laid down by her father's will: 'If I live to be as old as Sibylla, I will die as chaste as Diana' (Act 1 Scene 2, line 87). Ovid's *Metamorphoses* provided Shakespeare with the story of Sibylla, a prophetess who could live for as many years as the number of grains of sand she could hold. Diana was the goddess of chastity.

- As Morocco contemplates the lottery of the choice of caskets, he alludes to how 'Hercules and Lichas play at dice' (Act 2 Scene 1, line 32). Shakespeare may have found the story of Hercules playing dice in Plutarch's *Life of Romulus*. Lichas was Hercules' servant, who unwittingly provided him with a poisoned shirt. Hercules (Alcides is his Greek name – see Act 2 Scene 1, line 35) was driven mad when he wore the shirt. This is what Morocco imagines will happen to him if he makes the wrong choice of casket.

- Portia draws on another episode from the story of Alcides (Act 3 Scene 2, lines 53–62). She compares Bassanio to the heroic warrior who rescued Hesione from a sea monster in order to win a reward from her father, King Laomedon. Portia compares herself to the sacrificial virgin, Hesione. She imagines the onlookers as 'Dardanian wives' (women of Troy), weeping at the spectacle. The source for this tale is probably Ovid.

- Bassanio rejects the gold casket with the criticism that it is 'gaudy gold, / Hard food for Midas' (Act 3 Scene 2, lines 101–2). This refers to a story, in Ovid, about King Midas of Phrygia, who was granted his wish by Apollo that (literally) everything he touched should turn to gold.

- Lancelot, in dialogue with Jessica, explores her impossible dilemma as the daughter of two damned parents: 'thus when I shun Scylla your father, I fall into Charybdis your mother' (Act 3 Scene 5, lines 13–14). This refers to the story of Ulysses, who had to sail dangerously between the monster Scylla and the whirlpool of Charybdis, trying to avoid being ensnared by either hazard.

- At the beginning of Act 5 Shakespeare includes a catalogue of doomed lovers' partnerships, which undermines the playfully romantic mood of Jessica and Lorenzo. The stories are of Troilus (who was separated from, and betrayed by, his lover Cressida); of Thisbe (who never met her lover Pyramus); of Dido (the Queen of Carthage who was deserted by Aeneas); and of Medea (who ran away with her lover before he deserted her). Shakespeare probably came across some of the original tales in books by Chaucer. Others, such as Pyramus finding a blood-stained garment belonging to Thisbe and the story of Medea and Aeson, probably came from Ovid's *Metamorphoses*.

## What was Shakespeare's England like?

Shakespeare's audiences, watching performances of *The Merchant of Venice*, would recognise certain aspects of their own world. Many of those aspects were minor features of Elizabethan life, which they would have taken for granted.

A reference to 'my wealthy Andrew docked in sand' in Salarino's speech at the start of Act 1 has been taken by many as an allusion to the *San Andres*, a Spanish galleon captured by the Earl of Essex in Cadiz harbour in 1596. It was a wealthy prize and was taken into the English navy and renamed the *Andrew*. To Elizabethans it was probably a symbol of the kind of fortune that could be made and lost at sea. Further references to the 'Narrow Seas that part / The French and English' (the English Channel, where many trading vessels foundered) and 'the Goodwins' (a notorious sandbank six miles off the Kent coast), add to the topical details which confirm the dangers experienced by merchant sailors.

Portia's extensive list of suitors described in Act 1 Scene 2 is based on Elizabethan stereotypes of foreigners, reflecting commonly-held mistrust of other Europeans (England had relatively recently repelled the Spanish Armada). As noted on page 58, the word 'Scottish' was discreetly changed to 'other' by the time the First Folio was printed, since any satirical reference to the Scots was dangerous under King James I, himself a Scot.

The popular Elizabethan entertainment of masques is the backdrop to Jessica's elopement with Lorenzo. The masquers (the young Venetian gentry) prepare their disguises and their 'torch-bearers' as the prelude to an extravaganza of music and dance.

The play is rich in Elizabethan proverbs ('Hanging and wiving goes by destiny', 'Fast bind, fast find') as well as home-spun wisdom from Nerissa ('. . . they are as sick that surfeit with too much as they that starve with nothing'). Elizabethans saw Shylock's dream of money bags as a prediction that he was about to lose his money. Lancelot's confession that his 'nose fell a-bleeding' echoes another contemporary concern about ill omens.

Morocco describes an Elizabethan coin 'that bears the figure of an angel / Stampèd in gold' (it depicted the archangel Michael). Lorenzo speaks of the heavens decorated with 'patens of bright gold'. A 'paten' was a small dish or plate used in the Holy Communion, and the image probably reminded Shakespeare's audience of the gilded bosses of an elaborate Elizabethan ceiling, reflecting points of light.

Lorenzo, in speaking of the music of the heavens, draws on a contemporary belief that the concentric spheres (stars and planets) of the universe as defined by the astronomer Ptolemy actually produced music in the heavens as they gently collided with each other:

> There's not the smallest orb which thou behold'st
> But in his motion like an angel sings   (Act 5 Scene 1, lines 60–1)

Beyond such topical reminders of everyday life there are deeper ways in which *The Merchant of Venice* reveals what Elizabethan England was like. What follows identifies important social and cultural contexts that influenced the creation of the play: the history of the Jews, usury, the place of women in a patriarchal society, male friendship, cross-dressing, Venice and trade, the law, the Bible, revenge, and music.

## The history of the Jews
Although Antonio is the nominal hero of *The Merchant of Venice*, audience interest throughout the 400 years since the play was written has focused intensely on the character of Shylock.

At the time when Shakespeare sat down to write *The Merchant of Venice* there were probably still some Jews left in England, although they may have been reluctant to display their faith too conspicuously, as the critic James Shapiro explains:

> Perhaps a hundred or more Jews might have jostled
> Shakespeare in the crowded streets of London, and we know
> from Spanish Inquisition records and the complaints of various
> Catholic ambassadors, that Jewish holidays like Passover and

Yom Kippur were celebrated in England in the late sixteenth century.

The presence of the Jews in England dates back to the time of William the Conqueror, who had encouraged them to settle there after the Norman Conquest. In the twelfth century they were granted the right to manage and govern their own community according to their own laws and edicts, and they were publicly recognised by King John. There were sporadic outbursts against them, largely focused on unfounded accusations of attacks on children, and the papacy intervened in a plea for tolerance. This was largely granted during the reign of King Henry II, although the Jews were still excluded from joining the growing town guilds and from owning land.

One of the major factors in the tolerance of Jews was their significant contribution to the economic well-being of the country. The Christian Church was firmly set against the idea of money-lending, expressly forbidding the charging of interest on loans. In addition, there was no facility for the lending of money commercially within society. A group of comparatively wealthy Jews established themselves as money-lenders and provided a valuable service within society, a service that spread from the individual issuing of loans to providing a safety net to the rich and powerful landed gentry who had cashflow problems as they frequently struggled to collect their taxes.

So successful were the Jews in garnering their wealth that the government saw them as a legitimate and valuable target for further taxation. Thus they contributed covertly to the prosperity of the government. As they accumulated huge fortunes, several Jews became powerful and prestigious bankers.

Once their financial success became so marked, the Jews developed into increasingly attractive targets. Royals used Jewish money to support their lifestyle. All a Jew's assets, at death, were seized by the king and, with some irony given that they were still denied many of the basic rights of Christians, Jews were expected to support the Christian community through payment of church taxes. Their money was used primarily to fund King Richard I's crusades. Even though Jews made up a tiny minority of the population, they had a considerable influence on the financial state of the nation.

Yet by the end of the thirteenth century the Jews had largely been expelled from England. In 1290, in the reign of Edward I, they were officially exiled and they left in their thousands. The rise of other banking houses, such as the Italian Lombards, had marginalised Jewish money-lenders.

Worse still, English suspicion and bigotry against the Jews had gathered pace to such an extent that riotous protests against them had flared up. By 1217 they had been forced to wear the humiliating yellow badge that labelled their religious caste. To a contemporary English person the word 'Jew' was also a label, one that indicated a stereotypical version of a shifty profiteer who was not to be trusted.

Although the vast majority of the Jews were driven out of England in 1290, some of the more favoured ones were allowed to stay. Many settled in France, but there was a procession of Jewish refugees coming to England, fleeing persecution under the Inquisition in Spain.

The likely result, although no one can be sure, is that a sizeable number of Jews remained in England, many of them probably still privately adhering to the Jewish faith even though they were publicly professing to be Christian converts. Although there were Jews in England at the time Shakespeare created Shylock, scholars have found it difficult to identify any individuals who might have provided the original model for him.

What is likely, however, is that a contemporary event triggered Shakespeare's artistic imagination. In 1594, two or three years before the first performance of *The Merchant of Venice*, there was a high-profile trial and execution of a Jew called Roderigo Lopez. Lopez was physician to Queen Elizabeth, and was accused of attempting to poison her. There was great public interest in the case and considerable speculation about the extent of his plotting and scheming within the court. The trial and the gossip, in turn, sparked a hasty revival of Marlowe's *The Jew of Malta* (see page 61) which was staged in the days after Lopez's hanging.

As Toby Lelyveld says in *Shylock on the Stage*:

> Thus, when Shakespeare presented *The Merchant of Venice*, Shylock's outrageous behaviour came as no shock to the Elizabethans. They sided with the Christians in the play, whose terms of opprobrium for Shylock reflected the popular attitude. It was natural for them to accept the sentence that compelled Shylock to turn Christian. They hated his religion as much as they did that of a Jesuit or a Turk.

All kinds of myths and legends had grown up around the concept of Jewishness in the centuries before *The Merchant of Venice* was written. Jews were accused of spreading the Black Death by poisoning the water. Christians also feared that Jews were ritual murderers (see, for example, the tragic story of the child murder of Hugh of Lincoln in Chaucer's *The Prioress' Tale*).

It was widely believed that Jews abducted Christian boys, circumcised and then executed them. Their blood was supposedly used for a variety of bizarre ceremonies. Other, more extreme, legends grew up around the idea of Jewish cannibalism. Elizabethans were so anxious about the Jewish threat that when Shylock has the phrase 'cut off' inserted in the terms of the bond, it could easily have suggested to them cutting off Antonio's genitals.

A tradition had developed in medieval morality plays of stereotyping Jews and emphasising their villainous wickedness by making them grotesque and evil, dressed in black cloaks, horned hats, and carrying the badge of European Jewry, the yellow circle, on their costume. James Shapiro says:

> Again and again the Jewish man was constructed as a creature of the bodily fluids: spitting, stinking, menstruating, smearing faeces on Christian symbols, constantly falling into privies. In their androgyny, monstrosity, implication in local and unsolvable crimes, apostasy [abandoning one's religious faith or moral principles], secret rituals, 'Sabbath', and interest in sorcery and magic, the Jews resembled the other great marginal and threatening social group of the early modern period: witches.

Inevitably, a modern audience cannot be neutral about the presentation of Shylock. However, it seems likely that he was received in an atmosphere of contempt and scorn by an Elizabethan audience. Hatred of Jews was embedded in the social convention of the time and Shylock would have been played, perhaps either by Richard Burbage or Will Kempe, without sympathy or compassion. He was a perplexing hybrid of malice and ridicule – and extremely provocative.

## Usury

Some Jews who were left in England practised usury: the lending of money and charging interest on its repayment. In 1571 the business of money-lending had been made legal, although the law suggested that a ten per cent maximum interest should be charged.

The rich nobles had their wealth tied up in land, and after the Middle Ages they faced steeply rising costs and competition from the newly-monied merchant classes. Many were extravagant and failed to adapt. They turned to usurers to meet their expenses, often using their estates as security against a loan. Frequently, the money-lenders were able to confiscate that estate and thus the distribution of power gradually shifted. Many of the young gentry who visited Shakespeare's Globe Theatre would have been very conscious of the problems of debt.

There had been a growing upsurge in borrowing. Much of it was used to finance trading, which was becoming of paramount importance. As debt grew, the blame was put at the door of the money-lenders for advancing easy credit: and the money-lenders were traditionally Jews. Thus usury and Judaism were clearly linked. Christianity still forbade charging of interest. According to the teachings of the Greek philosopher Aristotle, it was beyond the laws of physics for money to spawn further money. Antonio picks up with disparagement the point about 'barren metal' breeding in Act 1 Scene 3.

Elizabethans condemned usurers much as their predecessors had done and viewed them as wolves, devils and heretics. Yet hypocrisy was at the core of Elizabethan economic practice. As an emergent economic power they depended on the money-lenders for the financial resources to underwrite their expansion. There was also an intrinsic tension between whether their old religion, so staunchly against usury, and the new capitalism were compatible. This is at the heart of Shylock's ambivalence. He remains both a 'devil' and the scapegoat for the Christians' own guilty feelings. Shakespeare will not let the audience forget this. He also asserts that money-lending is one of the only ways in which Jews were allowed to earn a living.

The long-held objection to money-lending at interest was denounced formally in 1572 in a text by Sir Thomas Wilson, entitled *Discourse on Usury*:

that ugly, detestable, and hurtful sin of usury . . . men have forgotten free lending, and have given themselves wholly to live by foul gaining, making the loan a kind of merchandise, a thing directly against all law, against nature, and against God.

Shylock is a Jew and a money-lender. Usury was alien to both the Christian and the traditional way of life. Antonio is a Christian whose first words to Shylock in the play suggest his direct opposition to usury: 'I neither lend nor borrow / By taking nor by giving of excess'. The direct conflict between the two practices is clear from the start.

## Women in a patriarchal society

In Venetian – and Elizabethan – society, husbands and fathers strictly controlled the lives of wives and daughters. *The Merchant of Venice* reflects the subordinate position of women in Elizabethan England. Women had limited personal autonomy, their status and roles were subject to the tyranny of patriarchy (rule by men). Their rights were restricted, legally, socially and economically.

Paternal authority, supported by civil law, was all-powerful. To defy it required courage and could invoke serious punishment. Disobedient sons were usually disinherited or exiled; wayward daughters were confined, sometimes at home or even in convents. The notion of father–daughter conflict was a recurring theme for Shakespeare: in *A Midsummer Night's Dream* (Egeus and Hermia); *Romeo and Juliet* (Capulet and Juliet); *Hamlet* (Polonius and Ophelia); *King Lear* (Lear and Cordelia); *Much Ado About Nothing* (Leonato and Hero); and *Cymbeline* (Cymbeline and Imogen).

In Elizabethan society the power that women had outside the family was limited by the rules of inheritance, ingrained traditions, and the prejudiced attitudes of the state, the law and the Church. Although powerful women were not unknown (King James' mother was Mary Stuart, queen of Scotland, and his immediate predecessor on the throne was Queen Elizabeth I) there was much concern about the position of women in society.

Venice is ruled entirely by men. Women have no role at all in trade, politics or the law. Patriarchy also rules Belmont. Portia is head of the household at the start of the play, but her father still controls her destiny, even from the grave: 'I may neither choose who I would, nor refuse who I dislike, so is the will of a living daughter curbed by the will of a dead father.' Even when she escapes from her father's will through Bassanio's choice of the lead casket, she subjects herself immediately to her new husband's authority:

> This house, these servants, and this same myself
> Are yours, my lord's. *(Act 3 Scene 2, lines 170–1)*

Portia is compliant to Bassanio's authority and sovereignty. Bassanio is 'her lord, her governor, her king' and she is thereafter known as 'Lord Bassanio's wife'.

The Renaissance ideal of womanhood suggested that women should live in a state of quiet obedience, their chastity preserved until a time convenient to their husbands. When Bassanio dutifully returns, with Gratiano, to assist Antonio in Venice, Portia's and Nerissa's lot is to 'live as maids and widows' until their husbands come back to Belmont.

In contrast to Portia, Jessica wilfully rejects her father's authority, rebelling against Shylock's apparent strictures ('Our house is hell'). She robs him of gold and jewels and elopes with a Christian, even becoming converted herself. Jewish communities would see this as the worst possible disaster that could befall a family, although Shylock's cry that he wishes she were dead, and buried with the ducats she stole, exceeds what even the most authoritative patriarchal figures in Elizabethan society might endorse.

## Male friendship

To an Elizabethan audience, the friendship between males in what was a predominantly patriarchal society would have been perfectly normal and acceptable. As Alan Sinfield notes:

> male friendship informed, through complex obligations, networks of extended family, companions, clients, suitors and those influential in high places.

Venice is almost completely characterised by friendships between men. At the core is the relationship between Antonio and Bassanio, which some critics view as homoerotic and the cause of Antonio's sadness at the start of the play.

The Christians are 'friends' but are largely a group of merchants and traders bound together by a group identity. They oppose the Jews and the Jewish practice of usury. They profit from trade. Solanio understands the concerns of a merchant whose ships are dangerously at sea:

> had I such venture forth,
> The better part of my affections would
> Be with my hopes abroad.  *(Act 1 Scene 1, lines 15–17)*

The Venetians are competitive and commercially-driven. They are also conscious of status and hierarchy within their group. Solanio introduces the arrival of Bassanio, Lorenzo and Gratiano with: 'We leave you now with better company.' They seem to have idle hours to spend: 'We'll make our leisures to attend on yours.' And Bassanio, at least, conforms to the Elizabethan model of a gentleman. Nerissa tells that he is a 'scholar and a soldier' although he has 'disabled' his estate and has 'great debts'.

Some critics (see pages 97–100) view the male friendship bonds as an important way of preserving the patriarchal system that underpins Venice. Karen Newman writes of 'the whole spectrum of bonds between men, including friendship, mentorship, rivalry, institutional subordination, homosexual genitality, and economic exchange' which are used to ensure that the males continue to dominate the Venetian way of life.

## Cross-dressing

On Shakespeare's stage, boy actors performed all the female parts. Contemporary audiences were used to this device and accepted males in female roles without question. This is a form of transvestism (literally 'cross-dressing') which was part of theatrical convention and would not have caused problems in, for example, the heightened romantic exchanges between Portia (played by a boy) and Bassanio. However, Shakespeare increases the complexity of this convention by including three versions of disguise which lead to boys playing the parts of women, who then dress up as men! This form of dramatic irony not only creates humour, but also contributes to the exploration of gender issues in *The Merchant of Venice*.

In order to escape from her father, Jessica disguises herself as a page, although she is 'much ashamed of my exchange'. When Lorenzo admires her dressed in the 'lovely garnish of a boy' he draws attention to the double disguise which Shakespeare's audiences might well have found amusing or delightful. The fact that she further decorates herself with 'moe [more] ducats' adds to the complexity of her deceptions.

Although cross-dressing was celebrated as a dramatic convention and 'homoeroticism is part of the fun of wooing' (according to the critic Alan Sinfield) the practice of such 'gross indecency' in Elizabethan life was frowned upon and prosecuted. It was condemned in virtually all religious and legal writing and it carried the death penalty although prosecutions were comparatively rare.

In order to compete in the male-dominated law courts of Venice, both Portia and Nerissa adopt the disguises of men. Portia mocks stereotypical male behaviour as she tells Nerissa of her plans. She laughingly tells Nerissa how she will be 'the prettier fellow' and carry her dagger more adroitly. There seems to be a clever joke by Shakespeare when he has Portia considering the pitch of her voice 'between the change of man and boy / With a reed [squeaky] voice'. Her speech continues to satirise accepted male habits like bragging, lying about love and fighting. Nerissa's 'Why, shall we turn to men?' is mischievously interpreted by Portia as questioning their sexual intent.

The courtroom was entirely the preserve of Elizabethan males, a place where they could display their mastery of the accepted masculine skills of logic, reasoning and rhetoric (the art of persuasion). Although there is no evidence that Portia has a legal background, she easily assumes the role of Doctor Balthazar and thereby enters the male world of law and politics. Portia ensures that the Venetian legal system survives, but contributes to the comic dénouement of the play by using her disguise to initiate the test of the rings.

## Venice and trade

England's role as a trading nation grew significantly during the latter part of the sixteenth century. The rise in the merchant classes saw a shift in power, and tensions began to emerge between the city entrepreneurs and the landed gentry. As the merchants tried to increase their wealth they took ever greater risks and the perils of trade were familiar to many of them. When Salarino speaks of imagined calamities at sea, he would have struck a chord with many traders in the audience.

*The Merchant of Venice* resounds with commercial language familiar to Shakespeare's contemporaries. To Elizabethans, Venice was a symbol of a trading centre which embraced many of the qualities of England of the 1590s, but also some significant differences. It was renowned as a city built on extensive trading links with Europe and beyond – Antonio's ships have sailed to 'Tripolis, from Mexico, and England, / From Lisbon, Barbary, and India' (as did English traders). Venice symbolised the balance between mercantile, capitalist ventures and the delicate preservation of social privileges going back centuries. It was opulent, a world-famous centre for banking. Perhaps most significantly, it was legendary for its tolerance of outsiders and had a reputation as a melting-pot for different cultures and minorities, especially entrepreneurs in business.

Shakespeare endows the Italian setting with many English values. The attitudes of the merchants at the start of the play reflect the attitudes of the English social groups. In comparing Antonio's ships to 'signors' (gentlemen) and 'rich burghers' (important citizens) Salarino shows every awareness of the hierarchy of class. Many of the Christians seem to have plenty of time for leisure and relaxation: they are not seen at business. Bassanio is an opportunist who depends on a rich friend and plans to repay his debts by speculation.

Belmont seems to reflect the Elizabethan ideal of the country retreat. Great aristocrats of Shakespeare's age were busy building such lavish country houses and using them to celebrate collections of artistic treasures and cultural experiences, such as the performance of music. Belmont is perhaps built on inherited wealth rather than commerce, but equally it may have been purchased with the profits of commercial enterprise, and it reflects the expansive estates built around Venice in Elizabethan times.

## The law

Elizabethans were fascinated by legal issues. Many of the audience in the Globe Theatre were likely to have been studying law at the Inns of Court in London. Many others were often involved in legal disputes. Shakespeare's contemporaries were extremely litigious, and delighted in the complexities of the legal system. Elizabethan plays were renowned for including trial scenes. Although Shylock's entitlement to his 'pound of flesh' is highly improbable, even when the mysterious setting of the Venetian courtroom with its own idiosyncratic laws is taken into account, the realism of the trial scene is gripping. Shakespeare's audiences would have found the trial scene as electrifying as modern audiences. They would also have relished the legal trickery displayed by Portia. Her meticulous attention to the letter of the law and the exact terms of the bond, allied to the more symbolic punishment of Shylock, probably pleased all elements of the audience.

Legal historians studying *The Merchant of Venice* have analysed the trial scene as an example of the two legal systems in operation in Shakespeare's day. Civil cases were settled in common law courts, based on precedents having been set. Cases that went to Chancery were decided by the Lord Chancellor's sense of natural justice (Shakespeare's parents had a case going through Chancery at the time when the play was being written). Some critics see the trial as an example of the Duke acting like the Lord Chancellor of England and dispensing 'equity', a form of justice where the judge resolved disputes based on established principles which were then adjusted to meet the specifics of the case.

Elizabethans were intrigued by the concepts of justice and judgement (Shakespeare later explored these searchingly in *Measure for Measure*). They relished the verbal and legal trickery which caught out the criminal and turned the tables on the villain. Shylock's traditional view of justice, a revenge which takes an eye for an eye, is refuted. Portia seems to try to ensnare Shylock before destroying him with the revelation of the loophole in the bond. Her supremely eloquent appeal for mercy does not sit comfortably with this strategy.

## The Bible

Elizabethans were used to hearing passages from the Bible read aloud every Sunday, as they had to attend their parish church or they were liable to be heavily fined. All educated Elizabethans were familiar with the written text. Shakespeare himself had to learn many of the psalms in his early years at school and he would have translated these into Latin when he went to grammar school. There is also evidence that he read from at least two versions of the Bible (the Geneva Bible and the Bishops' Bible).

There are many echoes of the Bible in *The Merchant of Venice*. Although Shakespeare may have known directly of Jews and their customs, it is thought that he also drew upon the stories of the Book of Genesis in creating some of the background to Shylock. The play contains references to Jacob, Laban's sheep and 'Hagar's offspring'. There are probably over 50 biblical allusions in the play:

- The word 'Nazarite' (Jesus of Nazareth) and 'conjured the devil into' (an echo of Matthew 8.28) (Act 1 Scene 3, line 28).
- 'The curse never fell upon our nation till now' (Act 3 Scene 1, lines 67–8). This probably reflects Matthew 23.8, referring to Christ's prophecy about the destruction of Jerusalem.
- The names Tubal and Chus, unlikely as names for Shylock's countrymen, are thought to have come from the Book of Genesis.
- When Shylock speaks of 'our holy Sabaoth' (Act 4 Scene 1, line 36) it echoes a phrase in the Te Deum: 'Holy, Holy, Holy, Lord God of Sabaoth'.
- Shylock's mention of 'the stock of Barabbas' (Act 4 Scene 1, line 292) brings to mind the Jewish thief released from crucifixion by Pontius Pilate when Christ was condemned to the cross.
- Lorenzo describes how heavenly music 'Still choiring to the young-eyed cherubins' (Act 5 Scene 1, lines 62–4) cannot be heard by humans ('this muddy vesture of decay'). The musical allusion is an echo of the Book of Common Prayer. The reference to humanity suggests the Book of Genesis and the notion that the body is made from the dust of the earth.

## Revenge

Revenge was a common and popular theme amongst Elizabethan dramatists. Although it was often seen as understandable, it was not forgivable. It was against the laws of Christian morality ('Vengeance is mine, saith the Lord, I will repay') and a sin against God. It was also a profoundly anti-social act. In *Hamlet*, Shakespeare explores the dilemma of a man who knows that he will be damned if he takes revenge against Claudius for killing his father. But if he does not, Claudius, as the king, will not be punished in the mortal world.

In *The Merchant of Venice*, Shylock is the victim of ancient racial and religious prejudice. Revenge becomes almost a tribal obligation. Yet he seeks to plot his revenge through the legal system that operates in Venice. At many points in the play Shylock maintains that what he seeks is within what the law stipulates:

> I crave the law,
> The penalty and forfeit of my bond.   *(Act 4 Scene 1, lines 202–3)*

## Music

Renaissance Italy had fuelled a huge interest in all realms of the arts and culture. Elizabethans found music very alluring. Besides the prevalence of religious and formalised secular music there was a growth of popular music (especially ballads) and dance. Many of Shakespeare's plays feature music, song and dance. The use of music, with the musicians often being positioned behind a curtained gallery, created specific ambiences.

Venice has no music except for the 'masque' (Act 2 Scene 4, line 22). It is the music which Shylock finds so unattractive and so typical of the Christians' showiness: 'the vile squealing of the wry-necked fife' and the sounds of 'shallow foppery' which grate so harshly against his own sobriety.

In contrast with this raucous noise is the ritualised, ceremonial music of Belmont: the trumpeted fanfares at the entrance of the suitors and the singer who performs an accompaniment to Bassanio's reflection about his choice of casket. In Act 5, Stephano and his group of musicians create the music to establish the romantic moonlit scene at Belmont which anticipates Portia's return. Lorenzo refers to the legendary, enchanting power of music which can 'draw her home'. He later describes the transforming effect that music can have on any listener, even wild young horses: 'Their savage eyes turned to a modest gaze / By the sweet power of music.'

# Language

Expressions from *The Merchant of Venice* have become universally known. Many phrases have passed into everyday speech: 'love is blind', 'The quality of mercy is not strained', 'blinking idiot', 'All that glisters is not gold', 'over and above', 'something tells me', 'It is a wise father that knows his own child', 'so shines a good deed in a naughty world', and many others.

But the language of the play is much more than a treasure house of quotations. It contains a wide variety of language registers. Its stylistic diversity can be seen by simply listing a few of these: Shylock's emotional pleas for understanding and his passionate exploration of the desire for revenge, his anguish at the loss of his daughter and his reviling of his Christian tormentors. There is racist bullying and coarse vulgarity from Gratiano. Lancelot Gobbo offers clever wordplay and riddling misunderstandings. Portia's speeches range from heightened eloquence to functional, legal language; from expressive and subtle rhetoric to barbed torment.

The play abounds in inventive imagery and witty wordplay, proverbs, literary, classical and biblical references, violent exclamations, artificial conceits and hyperbole. The style ranges from the formal language of the law court to the lyrical romance of the final act.

Ben Jonson famously remarked that Shakespeare 'wanted art' (lacked technical skill). But his comment is mistaken, as is the popular image of Shakespeare as a 'natural' writer, utterly spontaneous, inspired only by his imagination. Shakespeare possessed a profound knowledge of the language techniques of his own and previous times. Behind the apparent effortlessness of the language lies a deeply practised skill. What follows are some of the language techniques Shakespeare uses in *The Merchant of Venice* to intensify dramatic effect, create mood and character, and so produce memorable theatre. As you read them, always keep in mind that Shakespeare wrote for the stage, and that actors will therefore employ a wide variety of both verbal and non-verbal methods to exploit the dramatic possibilities of the language. They will use the full range of their voices and accompany the words with appropriate expressions, gestures and actions.

# Antithesis

Antithesis is the opposition of words or phrases against each other, as in Portia's command to Antonio in the trial scene: 'You must prepare your bosom for his knife' (Act 4 Scene 1, line 241). This setting of word against word ('your bosom' stands in vulnerable contrast to the menace of 'his knife') is one of Shakespeare's favourite language devices. He uses it extensively in all his plays. Why? Because antithesis powerfully expresses conflict through its use of opposites, and conflict is the essence of all drama.

In *The Merchant of Venice*, conflict occurs in many forms: Christian versus Jew, mercy versus justice, father versus daughter, usury versus venture trading, appearance versus reality. The atmosphere of Belmont is set in striking contrast to that of Venice. Antithesis intensifies the sense of conflict, and embodies its different forms. For example, in Lancelot's first appearance, his soliloquy shows him struggling to weigh the arguments of 'fiend' versus 'conscience': should he run away from Shylock's service, or stay?

> 'Budge!' says the fiend. 'Budge not!' says my conscience.
>
> *(Act 2 Scene 2, lines 14–15)*

Portia's 'quality of mercy' speech is full of antitheses, and Lorenzo's praise of music (Act 5 Scene 1, lines 71–88) similarly uses antitheses to contrast all kinds of troublesome things and qualities with the 'sweet power of music.' Antonio's description of Shylock bristles with antitheses. In his endeavour to question Shylock's integrity, he sets 'devil' against 'Scripture', 'evil soul' against 'holy witness' and so on:

> The devil can cite Scripture for his purpose.
> An evil soul producing holy witness
> Is like a villain with a smiling cheek,
> A goodly apple rotten at the heart.
> O what a goodly outside falsehood hath!
>
> *(Act 1 Scene 3, lines 90–4)*

The same theme of false appearance is explored in a long series of antitheses by Bassanio as he contemplates making his choice of caskets (Act 3 Scene 2, lines 73–107). He considers in turn law, religion, cowardice, courage and beauty. In each example he shows how vice can be concealed beneath a mask of virtue. The function of the antitheses is to lead him to the choice of the casket of lead, which, unlike gold and silver, does not falsely promise riches within. Two examples from his speech illustrate the antitheses:

> There is no vice so simple but assumes
> Some mark of virtue on his outward parts.
>
> *(Act 3 Scene 2, lines 81–2)*

> the beauteous scarf
> Veiling an Indian beauty      *(Act 3 Scene 2, lines 98–9)*

The second example also illustrates Elizabethan racial prejudice against dark-skinned foreigners, as it uses 'Indian' as a pejorative term.

## Imagery

*The Merchant of Venice* abounds in imagery: vivid words and phrases that help create the atmosphere of the play as they conjure up emotionally-charged mental pictures in the imagination or invite the mind to explore the similarities, differences and strangenesses of the language comparisons. Shakespeare seems to have thought in images, and the whole play richly demonstrates his unflagging and varied use of verbal illustration. Perhaps the most famous example is Portia's description of 'mercy'. Her opening lines depict mercy first as freely and gently falling like rain, bestowing heaven's blessing on giver and receiver alike. She then depicts mercy as more powerful than any earthly monarch, and as the most suitable attribute that any ruler can possess:

> The quality of mercy is not strained,
> It droppeth as the gentle rain from heaven
> Upon the place beneath. It is twice blest:
> It blesseth him that gives, and him that takes.
> 'Tis mightiest in the mightiest, it becomes
> The thronèd monarch better than his crown.
>
> *(Act 4 Scene 1, lines 180–5)*

On stage, Portia's imagery gains extra force when the Duke of Venice is presented as a mighty monarch seated upon a kind of throne. But early critics, such as Dr Johnson and John Dryden, were critical of Shakespeare's fondness for imagery. They felt that many images obscured meaning and detracted attention from the subjects they represented. However, over the past 200 years critics, poets and audiences have increasingly valued Shakespeare's imagery (sometimes called 'figures' or 'figurative language'). They recognise how he uses it to give pleasure as it stirs the audience's imagination, deepens the dramatic impact of particular moments or moods, provides insight into character and intensifies meaning and emotional force. Images carry powerful significance far deeper than their surface meanings.

A striking example is Shakespeare's use of musical imagery. As Bassanio prepares to make his choice of casket, Portia calls for music, so that 'if he lose he makes a swan-like end, / Fading in music' (swans were believed to sing as they died). In the play's final scene, Lorenzo points at the stars and uses an image based on the Elizabethan belief in the music of the spheres (see pages 50–1, 65):

> There's not the smallest orb which thou behold'st
> But in his motion like an angel sings   *(Act 5 Scene 1, lines 60–1)*

Lorenzo likens such heavenly music to the harmony 'in immortal souls', and later declares that a man 'that hath no music in himself' is utterly untrustworthy.

A profusion of similarly memorable word pictures pervade the play. Caroline Spurgeon, the critic best known for work on Shakespeare's imagery (see page 91) counted 113 images in *The Merchant of Venice*. That is a major underestimate. For example, she claims there are no images in Lancelot's encounter with Old Gobbo (Act 2 Scene 2, lines 25–92), but the episode contains 'sand-blind', 'gravel-blind', 'God's sonties' (saints), 'a hard way to hit' (difficult to find), 'raise the waters' (make him weep), and a dozen others, including 'truth will come to light', 'mine own flesh and blood', etc.

Some of the play's images appear to be highly embroidered and extravagant comparisons. Such images, full of hyperbole (exaggeration), are often referred to as 'conceits', which today tends to imply a negative evaluation. George Bernard Shaw, for example, spoke of the 'silly lyrical conceits which were the foible of the Elizabethans'. Perhaps the most striking and sustained conceit is Bassanio's praise of Portia's picture which he finds in the lead casket:

> Fair Portia's counterfeit! What demi-god
> Hath come so near creation? Move these eyes?
> Or whether riding on the balls of mine
> Seem they in motion? Here are severed lips
> Parted with sugar breath; so sweet a bar
> Should sunder such sweet friends. Here in her hairs
> The painter plays the spider, and hath woven
> A golden mesh t'entrap the hearts of men
> Faster than gnats in cobwebs. But her eyes –
> How could he see to do them? Having made one,
> Methinks it should have power to steal both his
> And leave itself unfurnished. Yet look how far
> The substance of my praise doth wrong this shadow
> In underprizing it, so far this shadow
> Doth limp behind the substance.    *(Act 3 Scene 2, lines 115–29)*

Bassanio's conceit is spun out over 15 lines. It is often judged as showy and ornamental, and so portraying insincerity rather than genuine emotions. But in Shakespeare's time, this high style of praise was both expected and valued as appropriate to the occasion. Today, it is sometimes regarded as Shakespeare self-indulgently showing off his language skills, picturing the painter as a 'demi-god'; as a 'spider' whose 'cobwebs' (Portia's hair) trap the hearts of men; and as threatened with blindness by the beauty of Portia's eyes.

Shakespeare's imagery uses metaphor, simile or personification. All are comparisons which in effect substitute one thing (the image) for another (the thing described).

- A simile compares one thing to another using 'like' or 'as', for example: 'laugh like parrots at a bagpiper', 'How like a fawning publican he looks!', 'It droppeth as the gentle rain from heaven', 'his affections dark as Erebus'.
- A metaphor is also a comparison, suggesting that two dissimilar things are interestingly similar. When Shylock says he would not

have given away Leah's ring 'for a wilderness of monkeys', the striking image stands for 'anything in the world'. Similarly, when Arragon leaves, his pride punctured by finding 'a portrait of a blinking idiot' in the silver casket, Portia uses a graphic image to describe what has happened: 'Thus hath the candle singed the moth.' Her words memorably signify that Arragon ('the moth') has been emotionally wounded ('singed') in his unsuccessful attempt to win Portia and her wealth ('the candle') which has so attracted him. To put it another way, a metaphor borrows one word or phrase to express another, for example when Shylock is described as a 'currish spirit', and 'wolfish, bloody, starved, and ravenous'. Shylock himself acknowledges the image, but accompanies it with a warning that uses the same imagery: 'Thou call'dst me dog before thou hadst a cause, / But since I am a dog, beware my fangs' (Act 3 Scene 3, lines 6–7).

The play is rich in images drawn from classical mythology (see pages 62–4). Bassanio's pursuit of Portia is compared to Jason's seeking the Golden Fleece at 'Colchos' strand'. Gratiano relates his and Bassanio's success at Belmont to that of the great heroic adventurer: 'We are the Jasons, we have won the fleece'. Portia is a worthy prize, likened to 'Cato's daughter, Brutus' Portia'(her husband, Brutus, was 'the noblest Roman of them all'). Portia's reputation is further strengthened when Shakespeare compares her to the revered prophetess Sibylla and to the goddess of chastity, Diana. Portia sees Bassanio as the heroic warrior, Hercules, who rescued Hesione (a sacrificial virgin) from a threatening sea monster. In the final act, Shakespeare draws on a list of doomed romantic partnerships to create an ominous mood: Troilus and Cressida, Thisbe and Pyramus, Dido and Aeneas, Medea and Aeson (see pages 49, 63–4).

## Repetition

The play has structural repetitions which increase its dramatic intensity (the three caskets, the trials and the 'rings' episodes). But repetition is most apparent in the play's language. Different forms of linguistic repetitions run through the play, contributing to its atmosphere, creation of character, and dramatic impact. Apart from familiar functional words ('the', 'and', etc.) the three words most frequently repeated are 'Jew' and 'Jews' (used nearly 70 times), 'bond' (around 40 times) and 'ring' (37 times). Their repetition is a clear indication of major preoccupations of the play.

Shakespeare's skill in using repetition to heighten theatrical effect and deepen emotional and imaginative significance is most evident in particular speeches. Repeated words, phrases, rhythms and sounds add intensity to the moment or episode. Repetition is a distinctive feature of Shylock's speech. Actors can use the repetitions effectively to convey different aspects of his character. For example, his careful, calculating mind is revealed in his first four speeches in the play:

| | |
|---|---|
| Three thousand ducats, well. | *(Act 1 Scene 3, line 1)* |
| For three months, well. | *(Act 1 Scene 3, line 3)* |
| Antonio shall become bound, well. | *(Act 1 Scene 3, line 5)* |

Three thousand ducats for three months, and Antonio bound.
*(Act 1 Scene 3, lines 8–9)*

The actor can, of course, use those lines to convey how much Shylock enjoys his power in this situation, as he deliberately keeps Bassanio waiting. The repetitions can be used as the actor chooses to convey an impression of Shylock's playful good humour or sinister coldness. Other repetitions reveal different aspects of his personality, for example his implacable insistence in Act 3 Scene 3 'I'll have my bond' (repeated five times in 13 lines); his anguish revealed in Solanio's report in Act 2 Scene 8 ('My daughter! O my ducats!'); and his joyfully repeated praise of Portia ('O wise young judge') throughout the trial scene as he thinks she will award him his bond (there are at least ten versions of this praise). Significantly, Gratiano uses the same repetitive style to mock Shylock when the tables are turned on him:

O upright judge!
Mark, Jew – O learned judge! *(Act 4 Scene 1, lines 308–9)*

Shylock's famous 'Hath not a Jew eyes?' speech has distinctive repetitions of words, phrases and rhythms (see page 113). His speech is in prose, but the same qualities of rhythmic and phrase repetition are found in the dialogue between Lorenzo and Jessica that begins Act 5, most obviously with the eight repetitions of 'In such a night'. But the dramatic purposes of the same style of repetition are quite different. Shylock passionately argues for common humanity of Jew and Christian. Lorenzo and Jessica lyrically call up a mythical past and romantic present.

Repetition also occasionally occurs in rhyme, which is used to achieve different effects. For example, the scrolls in the caskets are all in rhyme, giving them an incantatory, moralistic feel. Morocco's and Arragon's responses to the scrolls also rhyme, and the same sense of closure is evident as many scenes end with a rhyming couplet:

> Well, while I live I'll fear no other thing
> So sore as keeping safe Nerissa's ring.
>
> *(Act 5 Scene 1, lines 306–7)*

## Lists

One of Shakespeare's favourite language methods is to accumulate words or phrases rather like a list. He had learned the technique as a schoolboy in Stratford-upon-Avon, and his skill in knowing how to use lists dramatically is evident in the many examples in *The Merchant of Venice*. He intensifies and varies description, atmosphere and argument as he 'piles up' item on item, incident on incident. Sometimes the list comprises only single words, as in Gratiano's condemnation of Shylock ('wolfish, bloody, starved, and ravenous'), or Bassanio's description of Gratiano:

> Thou art too wild, too rude, and bold of voice
>
> *(Act 2 Scene 2, line 152)*

Other lists build up detailed descriptions, as in Nerissa's accounts of Portia's suitors in Act 1 Scene 2: the Neapolitan prince, the County Palatine, Monsieur Le Bon, Falconbridge, the Scottish lord, the young German.

Similar descriptive lists include Morocco's boasts (Act 2 Scene 1, lines 24–30) which ends with 'Yea, mock the lion when a roars for prey, / To win thee, lady'; Gratiano's amusing list of how he will behave respectably (Act 2 Scene 3, lines 160–8); and Shylock's grief for all he has lost, leaving him no satisfaction, no revenge, nor no ill luck stirring but what lights o'my shoulders, no sighs but o'my breathing, no tears but o'my shedding!                   *(Act 3 Scene 1, lines 74–6)*

But perhaps the most famous list in the play, packed with emotional and dramatic potential, is Shylock's passionate appeal to the common humanity of Jew and Christian:

Hath not a Jew eyes? Hath not a Jew hands, organs, dimensions, senses, affections, passions? Fed with the same food, hurt with the same weapons, subject to the same diseases, healed by the same means, warmed and cooled by the same winter and summer as a Christian is?
                                *(Act 3 Scene 1, lines 46–50)*

The many lists in the play provide valuable opportunities for actors to vary their delivery. In speaking, an actor usually seeks to give each 'item' a distinctiveness in emphasis and emotional tone, and sometimes an accompanying action and expression. In addition, the accumulating effect of lists can add to the force of argument, enrich atmosphere, amplify meaning and provide extra dimensions or perspectives to interpret and re-evaluate character.

## Verse and prose

About 80 per cent of the play is in verse, 20 per cent is in prose. How did Shakespeare decide whether to write in verse or prose? One answer is that he followed theatrical convention. Prose was traditionally used by comic and low-status characters. High-status characters spoke verse. Comic scenes were written in prose (as were letters, like Bellario's), but audiences expected verse in serious scenes: the poetic style was thought to be particularly suitable for moments of high dramatic or emotional intensity, and for tragic themes.

Shakespeare obviously used his judgement about which convention or principle he should follow in *The Merchant of Venice*. Thus Lancelot (low status) uses prose consistently. But both Portia (very high status) and Nerissa speak all of Act 1 Scene 2 in prose, perhaps because Shakespeare considered it a comic scene. Similarly, Lorenzo (high status) speaks prose in his dialogue with Lancelot in Act 3 Scene 5. Shylock, as a Jew, has low status in Venice, and many of his speeches are in prose. The fact that his 'Hath not a Jew eyes?' speech is in prose demonstrates that Shakespeare can use prose just as effectively as verse to express the deepest feelings and the most profound thoughts. Nonetheless, in the trial scene Shylock consistently uses verse, perhaps because the scene is serious, and he is in the company of high-status characters.

The verse of the play contains a relatively small number of rhymes, most notably in the casket scroll inscriptions, the song, and the couplets that end many scenes. But mostly the verse of *The Merchant of Venice* is blank verse: unrhymed verse written in iambic pentameter. It is conventional to define iambic pentameter as a rhythm or metre in which each line has five stressed syllables (/) alternating with five unstressed syllables (×):

> ×　/　×　/　×　/　×/　×　/
> How like a fawning publican he looks!

At school, Shakespeare had learned the technical definition of iambic pentameter. In Greek *penta* means 'five', and *iamb* means a 'foot' of two syllables, the first unstressed, the second stressed (as in the pronunciation of 'alas': aLAS). Shakespeare practised writing in that metre, and his early plays, such as *Titus Andronicus* or *Richard III* tend to be very regular in rhythm (de-DUM de-DUM de-DUM de-DUM de-DUM), and with each line 'end-stopped'(making sense on its own).

*The Merchant of Venice* is a fairly early play (1596–7), but with the experience of having written around a dozen plays, Shakespeare was becoming more flexible and experimental in his use of iambic pentameter. There is general critical agreement that a good deal of the play's verse achieves greater maturity of feeling than in earlier plays. The 'five-beat' rhythm is still often obvious, but at other times it is less prominent, notably in the 'balcony' scene in Act 2 Scene 6, when Jessica elopes with Lorenzo. End-stopped lines are less frequent. There is greater use of *enjambement* (running on), where one line flows on into the next, seemingly with little or no pause, as in the following speech of Lorenzo's:

> Here will we sit, and let the sounds of music
> Creep in our ears; soft stillness and the night

Become the touches of sweet harmony.
Sit, Jessica. Look how the floor of heaven
Is thick inlaid with patens of bright gold.

*(Act 5 Scene 1, lines 55–9)*

Some critics, directors and actors have strong convictions about how the verse should be spoken. For example, the director Peter Hall insists there should always be a pause at the end of each line. But it seems appropriate when studying (or watching or acting in) *The Merchant of Venice*, not to attempt to apply rigid rules about how the verse should be spoken. Shakespeare certainly used the convention of iambic pentameter, but he did not adhere to it slavishly. He knew the rules, but he was not afraid to break them to suit his dramatic purpose. No one knows for sure just how the lines were delivered on Shakespeare's own stage, and today actors use their discretion in deciding how to speak the lines. They pause or emphasise to convey meaning and emotion and to avoid the mechanical or clockwork-sounding speech that a too-slavish attention to the pentameter line might produce.

# Traditional criticism

Critical writing about *The Merchant of Venice* has always displayed awareness of the play's ambiguities and morally troubling aspects. For example, Nicholas Rowe in 1709 commented that although the play was usually played as a comedy, and Shylock portrayed as a comic character:

> . . . I cannot but think it was designed tragically by the author. There appears in it such a deadly spirit of revenge, such a savage fierceness and fellness, and such a bloody designation of cruelty and mischief, as cannot agree either with the style or characters of comedy . . .

But Rowe was also concerned to stress that the play was 'beautifully written'. His emphasis on the quality of the writing has been echoed by subsequent critics, sometimes to the neglect of the darker social implications of the play. Indeed, early critics often unequivocally sided with the Christians and condemned Shylock. For example, Francis Gentleman in 1770 comments that 'the retorts of Gratiano are admirably pleasant', and that Shylock is 'a most disgraceful picture of human nature . . . subtle, selfish, fawning, irascible and tyrannic'.

That negative interpretation of Shylock was reinforced by stage productions, but after seeing Edmund Kean's radically different performance in 1814, William Hazlitt acknowledged the 'error' of such a portrayal. He pointed to Shylock's 'strong grounds' for hating the Christians, noted the 'deep sense of justice' behind his resentment, and asserted:

> . . . we can hardly help sympathising with the proud spirit . . . we pity him, and think him hardly dealt with by his judges.

But Hazlitt's use of 'we' shows how inappropriate the use of the first person plural ('we', 'us', 'our') is in criticism. It is a style that has bedevilled critical writing for centuries (and still does today). Hazlitt was reporting his own personal response to the play. Right up to the present day, many have failed to share his sympathy for Shylock. But Hazlitt's comment has great significance because it displays one of the major features of traditional critical writing about the play: character criticism. Attention has increasingly focused on characters, often treating them as real people.

The critic with whom the expression 'character study' is most associated is A C Bradley. Around 100 years ago, Bradley delivered a course of lectures at Oxford University which were published in 1904 as *Shakespearean Tragedy*. The book has never been out of print, and Bradley's approach has been hugely influential.

Although Bradley only mentions *The Merchant of Venice* twice (he is centrally concerned with *Hamlet*, *Macbeth*, *Othello* and *King Lear*), his form of criticism reflects previous approaches to the play, and has strongly influenced critical approaches right up to the present day. It should also be noted that in his brief mention of the play Bradley also typically uses the highly misleading first person plural:

> . . . the end of *The Merchant of Venice* fails to satisfy us that
> Shylock is a tragic character . . . we cannot believe in his
> accepting his defeat and the conditions imposed on him.

Bradley talks of the characters in Shakespeare as if they were real human beings existing in worlds recognisable to modern readers. He identifies the unique desires and motives which give characters their particular personalities, and which evoke feelings of admiration or disapproval in the audience. Assuming that each character experiences familiar human emotions and thoughts, Bradley's presentation of conflict in Shakespeare's tragedies is primarily of conflict within the individual, an inward struggle.

Bradley's character approach has been much criticised, particularly for its neglect of the Elizabethan contexts of the play's creation: the cultural and intellectual assumptions of the time, stage conditions, and poetic and dramatic conventions. The section on Contexts demonstrates the powerful influence on *The Merchant of Venice* of such factors (pages 57–77). His brief judgement on Shylock (not 'a tragic character') is also contestable because notions of tragedy have expanded and changed from those Bradley assumed.

The most frequent objection to Bradley is his treatment of characters as real people. Modern criticism is uneasy about discussing characters in this way, preferring to see them as fictional creations in a stage drama. But although Bradley has fallen from critical favour, his influence is still evident. As pages 121–4 show, it is difficult to avoid talking or writing about characters as if they were living people and making moral judgements on them.

Following Bradley, and sharing his assumptions, Caroline Spurgeon opened up a fresh perspective on *The Merchant of Venice*: the study of its imagery. In her book *Shakespeare's Imagery and What it Tells Us*, Spurgeon identifies patterns of imagery in each of Shakespeare's plays. She finds *The Merchant of Venice* unusual in having a more uneven and varied distribution of images than any other play. Nonetheless, she remarks how the constant presence of music helps to create the play's atmosphere, and she notes that many images are drawn from nature, for example Gratiano's comment that some men's faces

> Do cream and mantle like a standing pond
>> *(Act 1 Scene 1, line 89)*

The value of Caroline Spurgeon's pioneering study of Shakespeare's imagery has been acknowledged by later critics, but her work has also been much criticised. She entirely overlooks the sexual images in *The Merchant of Venice* (for example, the Elizabethan use of 'ring' to imply female genitals). She very surprisingly claims there are no images in Lancelot's encounter with Old Gobbo (there are well over a dozen). She only occasionally examines how the imagery relates to the dramatic context of the play, and she sometimes makes speculative claims about the source of certain images, for example claiming that Bassanio's reference to a crowd's joyful reaction to 'some oration fairly spoke / By a belovèd prince' (Act 3 Scene 2, lines 178–9) is

> a little vignette surely drawn by an eyewitness of what must often have happened in Elizabethan London and its neighbourhood when the great queen was on her progresses.

A further criticism is that Spurgeon's tone is invariably one of praise, avoiding any negative appraisal of the play's imagery. In this she echoes the 'bardolatry' that has dogged Shakespeare criticism ever since the Romantics of the early nineteenth century. Other critics have been more sceptical, arguing that because Shakespeare wrote the play fairly early in his career he sometimes uses excessively elaborate imagery or 'conceits'. (You can find examples of conceits in the discussion of imagery on pages 81–2.)

Other critics have followed Spurgeon's example in paying detailed attention to the language of the play. G Wilson Knight was especially concerned with what he saw as the opposing imagery of tempest and music in the play. He makes much of the sea distance between Venice and Belmont, and argues that one is a place of tragedy, the other of love. He describes Shylock as a 'tempest', and in the romantic style that typifies so much traditional criticism, writes:

> But Portia, love's queen, descends from the fairyland of music
> and love, Belmont, into the turmoil and dust of human conflict
> and cruelty at Venice. She is as a being from a different world
> . . . she takes arms against the tragic forces of tempest and
> wins . . . It is the conquest of romance over tragedy, music and
> love's gold over tempests.

Other critical approaches have concentrated on identifying the themes and values of the play. Thus, much nineteenth- and twentieth-century criticism discusses issues of justice and mercy, male friendship, love and money. But the emphasis on character, and moral judgement of those characters is still evident, as for example in Muriel Bradbrook's claim that 'the characters are at the same time fully human, and symbolic or larger than human'. In support of her claim that the theme of the play is justice and mercy she asserts that

> Shylock, in so far as he stands for anything, stands for the Law
> . . . Portia's successful disguise, the nature of the bond itself,
> the set pleas of Justice and Mercy are all artifice, designed not
> to make the story slighter but to control, direct and focus the
> emphasis upon the theme or 'cause' of the play.

Harold Bloom is the most recent critic to write in the tradition of Bradley's character criticism. In *Shakespeare: The Invention of the Human*, Bloom argues that Shakespeare's characters provided the self-reflexive models by which human beings first acquired selves to reflect on (or to put it more simply, Shakespeare's characters first showed us how to think about ourselves). That enormous claim about the origin of our subjectivity is disputed by almost all scholars, many of whom are dismissive of Bloom's character study approach as gushing and exaggerated.

But Bloom is far from gushing about *The Merchant of Venice*. He makes provocative judgements. The play is 'a profoundly anti-Semitic work', and Shylock is no more than 'a comic villain'. Bloom praises the energy in Shylock's prose and poetry, but sees the play as belonging to Portia, whom he describes as 'at worst a happy hypocrite', 'a great charmer'. Other character criticisms abound. Bassanio is a lightweight 'glittering gold digger'. Gratiano reminds Bloom of 'Hitler's favourite newspaper editor'. Antonio expresses 'triumphant anti-Semitism'.

Bloom is scathing about Shakespeare's creation of Shylock, who 'has played an inglorious part in the history of the Jews'. He believes that Shylock should not be played sympathetically on stage, and asserts (ironically?) that he should be presented as 'a hallucinatory bogeyman, a walking nightmare flamboyant with a big false nose and red wig' as if he were Barabas in Marlowe's *The Jew of Malta*. Bloom, dismissive of the 'savagery' of Shakespeare's portrait of the Jew, declares that the Holocaust makes *The Merchant of Venice* unplayable. His conclusion is stark:

> It would have been better for the last four centuries of the Jewish people had Shakespeare never written this play.

## Modern criticism

Modern criticism argues that traditional approaches to *The Merchant of Venice*, with their focus on character, are too individualistic. The concentration on personal feelings ignores society and history, and so divorces literary, dramatic and aesthetic matters from their social context. Contemporary critical perspectives therefore shift the focus from individuals to how social conditions of Venice and Belmont (and Elizabethan England) are reflected in characters' relationships, language and behaviour. Modern criticism also concerns itself with how changing social assumptions at different periods of time have affected interpretations of the play.

Before examining particular examples of recent critical approaches to *The Merchant of Venice*, it is helpful to summarise the major features that such perspectives commonly share. Contemporary Shakespeare criticism:

- is sceptical of 'character' approaches (but often uses them – see pages 121–4);
- concentrates on political, social and economic factors (arguing that these factors determine Shakespeare's creativity and audiences' and critics' interpretations);
- identifies contradictions, fragmentation and disunity in the plays;
- questions the possibility of 'happy' or 'hopeful' endings, preferring ambiguous, unsettling or sombre endings (Antonio remains melancholy, Venice intolerant);
- produces readings that are subversive of existing social structures;
- identifies how the plays express the interests of dominant groups, particularly rich and powerful males;
- insists that 'theory' (psychological, social, etc.) is essential to produce valid readings;
- often expresses its commitment (e.g. to feminism, or equality, or political change);
- argues all readings are political or ideological readings (and that traditional criticism falsely claims to be objective);
- argues that traditional approaches have always interpreted Shakespeare conservatively, in ways that confirm and maintain the interests of the elite or dominant class.

The following discussion of recent critical approaches is grouped under particular headings (political, feminist, performance, psychoanalytic, postmodern). These groupings represent current critical trends. But there is often overlap between the categories, and to pigeonhole any example of criticism too precisely is to reduce its value and application.

## Political criticism

'Political criticism' is a convenient label for approaches concerned with power and social structure. Such approaches to *The Merchant of Venice* are less concerned with traditional discussions of character or love and friendship, mercy and justice, than with historical realities of anti-Semitism and capitalism, both in Shakespeare's time and our own. As such, it examines wealth, power and status in Venice and analyses how conflict – dramatic and real – springs from the condition of society itself. Political criticism asserts that Shylock's grievances, Antonio's attitudes and Portia's actions must be understood in the context of the social world of the play.

For most political critics anti-Semitism is the most troubling aspect of that society. The question 'Is *The Merchant of Venice* an anti-Semitic play?' perturbed critics throughout the twentieth century. The Holocaust gave the question terrifying relevance, and political criticism has given it sharper focus, arguing that anti-Semitism arises from the structures and values of Venetian society. As such, political criticism tends to be sceptical of more traditional critics like A D Moody, who have argued that the play is deeply ironic throughout, and all the characters, Jew and Christian, are equally intolerable and malign. Such an interpretation is seen as sidestepping the unavoidable question about the play.

Graham Holderness discusses how the play may have been understood in the 'basic, unreflective anti-Semitism' of Elizabethan England (see pages 65–8). Holderness is interested in the genre of the play, and points out that over the centuries it has been variously regarded as a comedy, a romance, and a tragedy. But even though he shows how such different categories have been justified, he concludes that today, people's views are 'inevitably coloured by the horrors of the Holocaust', and as such it is

> impossible to overlook such a presence within the text of an ideology that has proved in very recent history the source of immense cruelty and suffering.

Other critics have concentrated on the commercial values which structure Venice. In such readings, the play has been interpreted as a dramatic allegory of the triumph of merchant capitalism (Antonio's trading ventures) over usury (Shylock's lending money at interest). In this interpretation, Act 5 is seen as an idealised celebration of a merchant–capitalist utopia.

A different political interpretation is advanced by Elliot Krieger. In *A Marxist Study of Shakespeare's Comedies* Krieger argues that the play shows how the aristocratic class (Portia and Belmont) triumphs over the newly emerging bourgeoisie (Shylock and Venice).

Kiernan Ryan rejects such interpretations as reductive. For Ryan, the main conflict of society is 'the really central contradiction between a racist capitalism and humanity'. That means having a full awareness of the Holocaust and the history of Jewry in the twentieth century. Such an awareness recognises the power of Shylock's rebuke to the Jew-baiting Christians. For Ryan it displays 'an irresistible egalitarian attitude', and condemns discrimination of all kinds:

> If you prick us, do we not bleed? If you tickle us, do we not laugh? If you poison us, do we not die? And if you wrong us, shall we not revenge? If we are like you in the rest, we will resemble you in that. If a Jew wrong a Christian, what is his humility? Revenge. If a Christian wrong a Jew, what should his sufferance be by Christian example? Why, revenge! The villainy you teach me I will execute, and it shall go hard but I will better the instruction.          *(Act 3 Scene 1, lines 50–7)*

Ryan asserts that 'The villainy you teach me I will execute' vividly shows that Shylock's desire for revenge is not simply a result of his ill-treatment by the Christians. Rather, his bloodthirsty cruelty is the mirror image of their own true nature. That nature has been shaped by the money-centred society of Venice, and has similarly shaped Shylock. As such, his revenge is

> a bitter parody of the Christians' actual values, a calculated piercing of their unconsciously hypocritical facade.

Ryan sees the trial scene as similarly exposing those commercial values of Venice reflected in Shylock's behaviour: 'wolfish, bloody, starved, and ravenous'. But Ryan dismisses criticism which attempts to attribute blame between Shylock and the Christians. Rather, he argues that behind the apparent civilisation is a barbarity, the structural social forces of Venice which have shaped its citizens and authorise its prejudice and inhumanity:

> the ruthless priority of money values over human values, of the rights of property over the elementary rights of men and women . . .

And was Shakespeare himself anti-Semitic? Or did he write the play as a criticism of such intolerance and persecution? Ryan sees the play as 'Shakespeare's anguished rejection of the values invading Elizabethan England'. But no one knows for sure. Perhaps the most appropriate judgement is that of James Shapiro in his major book *Shakespeare and the Jews*. Shapiro concludes that Shakespeare wrote the play at a time when in England

> tolerance and equal, permanent status for Jews were not yet possibilities.

## Feminist criticism

Feminism aims to achieve rights and equality for women in social, political and economic life. It challenges sexism: those beliefs and practices which result in the degradation, oppression and subordination of women. Feminist critics therefore reject 'male ownership' of criticism, in which men determined what questions were to be asked of a play, and which answers were acceptable. They argue that male criticism often neglects, represses or misrepresents female experience, and stereotypes or distorts the woman's point of view.

Feminist criticism, like any 'approach', takes a wide variety of forms. Nonetheless, it is possible to identify certain major concerns for feminist critical writing on *The Merchant of Venice*. Most commonly, feminists approach the play using the notion of patriarchy (male domination of women). Feminists point to the fact that throughout much of history, power has been in the hands of men, both in society and in the family. *The Merchant of Venice* clearly reflects that patriarchal control, and feminists see the issue of unjust male power and control as crucial to understanding Belmont and Venice. In Belmont, Portia may be in charge of her household, but her freedom is restricted by her dead father. Even in death, through the trial of the caskets, he controls who she must marry. Portia feelingly expresses her dilemma:

> O me, the word 'choose'! I may neither choose who I would,
> nor refuse who I dislike, so is the will of a living daughter
> curbed by the will of a dead father.   *(Act 1 Scene 2, lines 19–21)*

In Venice, Shylock orders his daughter Jessica to shut up the doors and windows against the sounds of merriment. Her words express her experience with her father ('Our house is hell'), and in rebellion she steals his money as she elopes with Lorenzo. But Jonathan Miller's 1970 production showed that she fared little better at the hands of her husband, because in that performance all Lorenzo's words to her were spoken as pompous and condescending lectures, rather than in affection. Jessica's elopement can be seen as an act of feminine resistance against male oppression. But Jessica is often shown on stage as being treated by the Christian men and women alike with contemptuous disdain or casual indifference. Such an interpretation undermines the notion of female solidarity and resistance, which feminist critics argue can be seen in the play. Those qualities are most obviously seen in the way in which Portia and Nerissa assume male disguise and become powerful figures both in judicial affairs in Venice (defeating Shylock), and in shifting the balance of power with their husbands (through the 'rings' episode).

It is significant that the Christian society of Venice has no female characters. The two females who enter from Belmont must disguise themselves as males in order to be accepted as figures of authority. Even though Portia also seems very much in control in the final scene on her return to Belmont, feminist critics identify in the play a crucial problem for women's equality with men: the way Portia, like a stereotypical Elizabethan wife, gives everything, and herself, to Bassanio, and accepts him as her lord:

> This house, these servants, and this same myself
> Are yours, my lord's.               *(Act 3 Scene 2, lines 170–1)*

Karen Newman asserts that in the play women are regarded, like ships' cargoes, as goods for exchange. She disputes the view that Belmont is solely a place of love. Rather, she argues, it shares the same commercial values as Venice, as evidenced in both the matter and the mottoes of the caskets. Using a concept from anthropology, Newman argues that Venice and Belmont are characterised by the same 'structure of exchange'. That concept is based on the theory that marriage is the most fundamental form of gift exchange: men trading women, and through that exchange establishing bonds of male friendship. Newman sees the same process at work in the way Portia's father uses the caskets to give her to Bassanio. She argues that the 'bond' plot arises from this 'traffic in women', and that the exchange promotes and secures bonds of male friendship between Bassanio and Antonio. For Newman, Portia is the object of exchange, not a partner in it, as she submits to Bassanio:

> to be directed
> As from her lord, her governor, her king.
> Myself, and what is mine, to you and yours
> Is now converted.                    (Act 3 Scene 2, lines 164–7)

In this speech of submission, Newman detects the Elizabethan 'sex/gender system' in which wives were required to be obedient to their husbands, lost their legal rights, and became like goods or chattels (see page 70). But Newman's feminist concern is to show that although Portia seems to acquiesce to low status in the male-dominated system, she actually challenges and subverts male authority. She becomes an 'unruly woman', transgressing the Renaissance ideal of a proper lady. She dresses as a man, and in this male disguise is powerfully effective in her use of legal and logical language (traditionally regarded as male preserves). As such, Portia gives a 'gift' to Venice by preventing the disruption that Shylock's bond threatens. Further, in an exchange of her own, Portia uses her ring as a gift, seemingly as a visual sign of her love and submission. But the ring serves to discomfort Bassanio, and the play ends with Portia very much in control at Belmont.

In this feminist reading, Newman concludes that the play is subversive of the attitudes and values of Shakespeare's times:

> Far from exemplifying the Elizabethan sex/gender system of exchange, *The Merchant* short-circuits the exchange, mocking its authorised social structure and hierarchical gender relations . . .

Catherine Belsey also shares this view of the play as 'deeply socially disruptive in its challenge to the patriarchal order'. Belsey is particularly concerned with the 'rings' episodes in Acts 4 and 5, and the moment when Bassanio declares he would lose everything, including his wife, to save the life of his friend, Antonio. Belsey's interpretation of the episodes is based on the claim that at the time the play was written, notions of marriage were changing. For Belsey (like

Ryan – see page 96) the business of the rings suggests these new possibilities of male–female relationships. It opens up a utopian vision of marriage in which women share equal rights with men, and where the terms 'wife' and 'friend' include each other.

Feminists draw attention to other episodes and language that are often overlooked or played down by many male critics. Examples include the troubling allusions to unhappy love and broken vows, such as Portia's threat to sleep with the 'lawyer' to whom Bassanio gave her love-ring:

> I'll not deny him anything I have,
> No, not my body, nor my husband's bed
>
> *(Act 5 Scene 1, lines 227–8)*

They also marginalise the references to examples of male bonding and friendship such as the moment when Antonio bids farewell to Bassanio and 'with affection wondrous sensible . . . wrung Bassanio's hand' or the point in the trial scene where he urges Bassanio to 'say how I loved you'. Like all critical interpretations, such readings raise the question of whether they are what Shakespeare intended, but it must be noted that many critics today argue that Shakespeare's intentions can never be known.

## Performance criticism

Performance criticism fully acknowledges that *The Merchant of Venice* is a play: a script to be performed by actors to an audience. It examines all aspects of the play in performance: its staging in the theatre or on film and video. Performance criticism focuses on Shakespeare's stagecraft and the semiotics of theatre (words, costumes, gestures, etc.), together with the 'afterlife' of the play (what happened to *The Merchant of Venice* after Shakespeare wrote it). That involves scrutiny of how productions at different periods have presented the play. As such, performance criticism appraises how the text has been cut, added to, rewritten and rearranged to present a version judged appropriate to the times.

*The Merchant of Venice* seems to have been a popular play right from the time it was first performed, probably in 1597. The title page of the First Quarto (see page 57) claimed that it was performed many times by Shakespeare's acting company. It seems very likely that King

James saw the play twice in 1605. But few records exist of actual performances over the next 100 years, and in 1701 it was rewritten by George Granville, who called his version *The Jew of Venice*. Granville removed Lancelot, Old Gobbo, Morocco, Arragon, Tubal and some other characters. He cut and rearranged scenes, and added his own lines. Most notably, he included a spectacular banquet scene, in which Shylock was entertained by Antonio and Bassanio, and an impressive masque was performed. In the trial scene, Bassanio draws his sword in an attempt to prevent a verdict.

Granville's version held the stage for 40 years, and it was not until 1741 that London audiences again saw Shakespeare's own play. It was quite heavily cut, and several songs were added, but perhaps most striking was the portrayal of Shylock by Charles Macklin. It seems likely that up to 1741 Shylock was played as a comic figure, a buffoon with a flaming red beard. But Macklin played him as a terrifying villain, brooding and malevolent, determined on revenge. That conception of Shylock became the accepted style of performance until 1814 when Edmund Kean transformed the role.

Kean's Shylock was a sympathetic portrayal, described by the critic Hazlitt as 'a man more sinned against than sinning' (a line from *King Lear*). Kean's interpretation has influenced stage performances and criticism right to the present day, as actors and critics acknowledge the complexity of Shylock's character (see pages 122–3) as persecuted, villainous and dignified. Nineteenth-century productions became increasingly spectacular. Elaborate scenery and costumes, full of period detail, attempted to create an illusion of a historically 'authentic' Venice and a romantically idealised Belmont. Music, dance, even gondolas and canals, together with many 'extras' commonly featured to create an impression of Venetian carnival.

But Shylock continued to dominate the play, and at the close of the century Henry Irving's portrayal of him as a tragic figure was greatly admired, as the words of one contemporary theatre critic suggest:

> His Jew was no doubt often repulsive, but he had moments of sheer humanity, when one felt with him and almost, or quite, suffered with him.

The twentieth century saw a return to much simpler stagings of the play. Although the tradition of extravagant productions lingered on, most no longer attempted to create an impression of realism. Under the influence of William Poel and Harley Granville-Barker the stage was cleared of the clutter of historical detail. The aim was to recapture the conditions of the Elizabethan bare stage, which was not dependent on theatrical illusion. That implied a minimum of scenery, scenes flowing swiftly into each other, and a concern for clear speaking of Shakespeare's language. Poel returned to the earliest view of Shylock, regarding him as a malicious villain to be played in the old style, complete with red wig. However, Poel was writing in the early years of the twentieth century, and his evident unawareness of (or reluctance to address) the social issues of the play was a familiar characteristic of performance criticism. That neglect or avoidance of anti-Semitism is equally starkly revealed, but in different form, in Harley Granville-Barker's performance criticism.

In his *Prefaces to Shakespeare*, Granville-Barker, himself a playwright and director, conducts the reader through *The Merchant of Venice*, giving prescriptive advice on staging and characterisation. But his opening assertion, first made in 1930, symbolises the vast gulf between criticism written before and after the Holocaust:

> *The Merchant of Venice* is a fairy tale. There is no more reality in Shylock's bond and the Lord of Belmont's will than in Jack and the Beanstalk . . . *The Merchant of Venice* is the simplest of plays.

Granville-Barker is right to recognise that the play is, like all drama, a fictional creation. But the terrible crimes that Hitler committed upon the Jews has made it impossible for any serious stage version after 1945 to perform *The Merchant of Venice* with such blithe unawareness of history. The Holocaust has rendered the play anything but a fairy tale, and made it the most difficult of Shakespeare's plays.

Particularly in the closing decades of the twentieth century, and in the twenty-first, productions have been alert to the problematic nature of the play. Productions have tended to move away from very romantic portrayals of Belmont, choosing instead to emphasise the unpleasant social aspects of the play, particularly the brutal intolerance of anti-Semitic Venice. In a number of productions Shylock is spat upon by the Christians and reviled or assaulted in other ways. In one production he was constantly ridiculed, jostled and beaten. The audience saw street urchins hound and pelt him with stones. The victorious Christians wrestled him to the floor at the end of the trial scene.

Jonathan Miller's 1970 production treated Shylock sympathetically, cutting some speeches (for example, the entire aside that begins 'I hate him for he is a Christian' and 'I did dream of money bags tonight'). During the scene with Tubal, Shylock carried Jessica's dress over his arm. At the end of the trial scene he had a seizure or stroke. In different portrayals, Patrick Stewart played him as a miser who slapped Jessica's face at one point. David Suchet hugged and kissed his daughter. Ian McDiarmid gave her the ring, which she later squandered. Antony Sher's 1987 Shylock presented him as an anti-Semitic stereotype, a Middle Eastern Jew whose blood rituals, fanaticism and vulgarity marked him as an alien figure. Similarly, the BBC production of 1980 established him as unassimilated, gloating over his bond in the trial and waving his knife threateningly at his victim. The Christians responded in equally brutal style, forcing him to wear, and to kiss, a cross after his conversion.

*The Merchant of Venice* has been performed all around the world. There is a record of a performance in the USA in 1752, and in the nineteenth century the black American Ira Aldridge was much acclaimed. There have been several productions in Israel, all attracting controversy, especially around the issue of Shylock's enforced conversion. A German production in Weimar in 1995 set the play in a Nazi concentration camp. The Christians were played by the camp guards, and Shylock, Jessica and Tubal were played by three Jewish prisoners. The Morocco scenes were blatantly parodied as a racial caricature, and the Jews were murdered at the end. It is significant that the production was directed by an Israeli and the notorious concentration camp Buchenwald lies only a few miles from Weimar.

In 2000, the Royal National Theatre production of the play set it in the early 1930s. It transfers the action to a location that is more like Berlin than Venice, and thus draws on a modern audience's awareness of Nazi Germany, the Holocaust and the continual oppression endured by Shylock and his people. Henry Goodman's portrayal of Shylock underlined his villainy but tried to explore how the vicious abuse he has suffered has shaped his character. He is seen as an individual rather than simply a representative of his race.

## Psychoanalytic criticism

In the twentieth century, psychoanalysis became a major influence on the understanding and interpretation of human behaviour. The founder of psychoanalysis, Sigmund Freud, explained personality as the result of unconscious and irrational desires, repressed memories or wishes, sexuality, fantasy, anxiety and conflict. Freud's theories have had a strong influence on criticism and stagings of Shakespeare's plays, most obviously on *Hamlet*, in the well-known claim that Hamlet suffers from an Oedipus complex.

*The Merchant of Venice* has also evoked a good deal of psychoanalytic critical writing, perhaps, as Norman Holland speculates, because many psychoanalysts are Jewish. Holland's book, *Psychoanalysis and Shakespeare*, details a number of psychoanalytic interpretations of which the following are a representative selection:

- The caskets test represents an incest theme: Portia's father secretly desired her himself.
- Failure to solve the riddle of the caskets signifies castration: the loss of manhood.
- The caskets symbolise the requirement in some cultures for a man to refrain from intercourse on his wedding night.
- The Christians secretly fear the Jewish rite of circumcision. Shylock's demand for his bond is equivalent to the circumcision of Antonio. This implies that Antonio would become a Jew, and so is the motivation for the demand that Shylock convert to Christianity.
- Antonio personifies Christ and other dying gods in religion and mythology.
- The pound of flesh plot is related to childhood fantasies about suckling.
- The deepest level of the play is oral: Belmont, 'beautiful mountain', symbolises the bountiful mother breast.
- The exact measurement of the pound of flesh and the legal language of the trial scene typify anal traits.
- Antonio is 'father' to Bassanio, but through his ordeal becomes his 'son'.
- Shylock represents a bad, castrating father; Portia, a good, loving mother.
- Shylock's impulses reflect the infantile violence of childhood fantasies.

- Antonio's melancholy is Shakespeare's own sadness.
- Shylock has an outstanding characteristic of the anal–erotic personality: a tendency to hoard money, feeling that such possession gives power and control.

All these interpretations reveal the obvious weaknesses in applying psychoanalytic theories to *The Merchant of Venice*: they cannot be proved or disproved, they neglect historical and social factors, and they are highly speculative. Psychoanalytic approaches are therefore often accused of imposing interpretations based on theory rather than upon Shakespeare's text. Nonetheless, the play has obvious features which seem to invite psychoanalytic approaches: the pervading presence of aggression, particularly oral ('beware my fangs', etc.); the obsession with money and hoarding; the ordeals of the caskets and the trial scene; and the intense friendship of Antonio and Bassanio (see page 71).

## Postmodern criticism

Because *The Merchant of Venice* has become such a politically-charged play, critics who use postmodern techniques tend to avoid writing about it. Postmodern criticism (sometimes called 'deconstruction') is not always easy to understand because it is not centrally concerned with consistency or reasoned argument. It does not accept that one section of the story is necessarily connected to what follows, or that characters relate to each other in meaningful ways. Because of such assumptions, postmodern criticism is sometimes described as 'reading against the grain' or less politely as 'textual harassment'. The approach therefore has obvious drawbacks in providing a model for examination students who are expected to display reasoned, coherent argument, and respect for the evidence of the text.

Postmodernism often revels in the cleverness of its own use of language, and accepts all kinds of anomalies and contradictions in a spirit of playfulness or 'carnival'. It abandons any notion of the organic unity of the play, and rejects the assumption that a Shakespeare play possesses clear patterns or themes. Some postmodern critics even deny the possibility of finding meaning in language. They claim that words simply refer to other words, and so any interpretation is endlessly delayed (or 'deferred' as the deconstructionists say).

Other critics focus on minor or marginal characters, or on gaps or silences in the play. They claim that these features, previously overlooked as unimportant, reveal significant truths about the play. For example, Kim Hall bases a complex argument about gender, race, religion and money on a character who never appears: the Moor who Lancelot has made pregnant. Hall argues that the 'unheard, unnamed, and unseen' black woman is 'a silent symbol for the economic and racial politics of *The Merchant of Venice*'.

Postmodern critics make much of what they call 'the instability of language' . In practice, this often means little more than traditional notions of ambiguity: that words can have different meanings. It has long been accepted that Shakespeare's language has multiple, not single meanings. In *The Merchant of Venice*, that openness to multiple meanings is perhaps most clearly seen in the inscriptions on the caskets, which Morocco, Arragon and Bassanio interpret in very different ways – gold: 'Who chooseth me, shall gain what many men desire'; silver: 'Who chooseth me, shall get as much as he deserves'; lead: 'Who chooseth me, must give and hazard all he hath.'

Postmodern approaches to *The Merchant of Venice* are most clearly seen in stage productions. There, you could think of it as simply 'a mixture of styles'. The label 'postmodern' is applied to productions which self-consciously show little regard for consistency in character, or for coherence in telling the story. Characters are dressed in costumes from very different historical periods, and carry both modern and ancient weapons. Ironically, Shakespeare himself has been regarded as a postmodern writer for the way he mixes genres in his plays, combining comedy with tragedy.

# Organising your responses

The purpose of this section is to help you improve your writing about *The Merchant of Venice*. It offers practical guidance on two kinds of tasks: writing about an extract from the play and writing an essay. Whether you are answering an examination question, preparing coursework (term papers), or carrying out research into your own chosen topic, this chapter will help you organise and present your responses.

In all your writing, there are three vital things to remember:

- *The Merchant of Venice* is a play. Although it is usually referred to as a 'text', *The Merchant of Venice* is not a book, but a script intended to be acted on a stage. So your writing should demonstrate an awareness of the play in performance as theatre. That means that you should always try to read the play with an 'inner eye', thinking about how it could look and sound on stage. By doing so, you will be able to write effectively about Shakespeare's language and dramatic techniques.

- *The Merchant of Venice* is not a presentation of 'reality'. It is a dramatic construct in which the playwright, through theatre, engages the emotions and intellect of the audience. The characters and story may persuade the audience to suspend its disbelief for several hours. The audience may identify with the characters, be deeply moved by them, and may think of them as if they are living human beings. However, when you write, a major part of your task is to show how Shakespeare achieves the dramatic effects that so engage the audience. Through discussion of his handling of language, character and plot, your writing reveals how Shakespeare uses themes and ideas, attitudes and values, to give insight into crucial social, moral and political dilemmas of his time – and yours.

- How Shakespeare learned his craft. As a schoolboy, and in his early years as a dramatist, Shakespeare used all kinds of models and frameworks to guide his writing. But he quickly learned how to vary and adapt the models to his own dramatic purposes. This chapter offers frameworks that you can use to structure your writing. As you follow them, follow Shakespeare's example! Adapt them to suit your own writing style and needs.

# Writing about an extract

It is an expected part of all Shakespeare study that you should be able to write well about an extract (sometimes called a 'passage') from the play. An extract is usually between 30 and 70 lines long, and you are invited to comment on it. The instructions vary. Sometimes the task is very briefly expressed:

- Write a detailed commentary on the following passage.
  or
- Write about the effect of the extract on your thoughts and feelings.

At other times a particular focus is specified for your writing:

- With close reference to the language and imagery of the passage, show in what ways it helps to establish important issues in the play.
  or
- Analyse the style and structure of the extract, showing what it contributes to your appreciation of the play's major concerns.

In writing your response, you must of course take account of the precise wording of the task, and ensure you concentrate on each particular point specified. But however the invitation to write about an extract is expressed, it requires you to comment in detail on the language. You should identify and evaluate how the language reveals character, contributes to plot development, offers opportunities for dramatic effect, and embodies crucial concerns of the play as a whole. These 'crucial concerns' are also referred to as 'themes', or 'issues', or 'preoccupations' of the play.

The following framework is a guide to how you can write a detailed commentary on an extract. Writing a paragraph or more on each item will help you bring out the meaning and significance of the extract, and show how Shakespeare achieves his effects.

**Paragraph 1:** Locate the extract in the play and say who is on stage.
**Paragraph 2:** State what the extract is about and identify its structure.
**Paragraph 3:** Identify the mood or atmosphere of the extract.

**Paragraphs 4–8:**
  Diction (vocabulary)
  Imagery
  Antithesis
  Repetition
  Lists

These paragraphs analyse how Shakespeare achieves his effects. They concentrate on the language of the extract, showing the dramatic effect of each item, and how the language expresses crucial concerns of the play.

**Paragraph 9:** Staging opportunities
**Paragraph 10:** Conclusion

The following example uses the framework to show how the paragraphs making up the essay might be written. The framework headings (in bold) would not, of course, appear in your essay. They are presented only to help you see how the framework is used.

## Extract

SOLANIO    Let me say 'amen' betimes, lest the devil cross my prayer, for here he comes in the likeness of a Jew.

    *Enter* Shylock

How now, Shylock, what news among the merchants?

SHYLOCK    You knew, none so well, none so well as you, of my daughter's flight.

SALARINO    That's certain; I for my part knew the tailor that made the wings she flew withal.

SOLANIO    And Shylock for his own part knew the bird was fledged, and then it is the complexion of them all to leave the dam.

SHYLOCK    She is damned for it.

SALARINO    That's certain – if the devil may be her judge.

SHYLOCK    My own flesh and blood to rebel!

SOLANIO    Out upon it, old carrion! Rebels it at these years?

SHYLOCK    I say my daughter is my flesh and my blood.

SALARINO    There is more difference between thy flesh and hers than between jet and ivory; more between your bloods than there is between red wine and Rhenish. But tell us, do you hear whether Antonio have had any loss at sea or no?

SHYLOCK    There I have another bad match: a bankrupt, a prodigal, who dare scarce show his head on the Rialto, a beggar that was used to come so smug upon the mart. Let him look to his bond. He was wont to call me usurer; let him look to his bond. He was wont to lend money for a Christian courtesy; let him look to his bond.

SALARINO    Why, I am sure if he forfeit thou wilt not take his flesh. What's that good for?

SHYLOCK    To bait fish withal; if it will feed nothing else, it will feed my revenge. He hath disgraced me, and hindered me half a million, laughed at my losses, mocked at my gains, scorned my nation, thwarted my bargains, cooled my friends, heated mine enemies – and what's his reason? I am a Jew. Hath not a Jew eyes? Hath not a Jew hands, organs, dimensions, senses, affections, passions? Fed with the same food, hurt with the same weapons, subject to the same diseases, healed by the same means, warmed and cooled by the same winter and summer as a Christian is? If you prick us, do we not bleed? If you tickle us, do we not laugh? If you poison us, do we not die? And if you wrong us, shall we not revenge? If we are like you in the rest, we will resemble you in that. If a Jew wrong a Christian, what is his humility? Revenge. If a Christian wrong a Jew, what should his sufferance be by Christian example? Why, revenge! The villainy you teach me I will execute, and it shall go hard but I will better the instruction.

*Enter a Servingman from Antonio*

SERVINGMAN    Gentlemen, my master Antonio is at his house, and desires to speak with you both.

SALARINO    We have been up and down to seek him.

*Enter Tubal*

SOLANIO  Here comes another of the tribe; a third cannot be matched, unless the devil himself turn Jew.

*Exeunt Salarino and Solanio with the Servingman*

SHYLOCK    How now, Tubal, what news from Genoa? Hast thou found my daughter?

TUBAL    I often came where I did hear of her, but cannot find her.

SHYLOCK    Why there, there, there, there! A diamond gone cost me two thousand ducats in Frankfurt! The curse never fell upon our nation till now, I never felt it till now. Two thousand ducats in that, and other precious, precious jewels! I would my daughter were dead at my foot, and the jewels in her ear: would she were hearsed at my foot, and the ducats in her coffin. No news of them, why so? And I know not what's spent in the search. Why thou loss upon loss – the thief gone with so much, and so much to find the thief, and no satisfaction, no revenge, nor no ill luck stirring but what lights o'my shoulders, no sighs but o'my breathing, no tears but o'my shedding!                    *(Act 3 Scene 1, lines 17–76)*

**Paragraph 1: Locate the extract in the play and say who is on stage.**
Jessica, having plundered her father's gold and jewels, has eloped with Lorenzo. Shylock has searched unavailingly for the couple and has reacted passionately to the loss of his wealth and his daughter. He knows that one of Antonio's trading ships has gone down in the English Channel. Shylock is about to confront the Christians, Solanio and Salarino, and accuse them of complicity in the flight of his daughter. Tubal will brief Shylock on the latest he has been able to find out about Jessica.

**Paragraph 2: State what the extract is about and identify its structure.**
(Begin with one or two sentences identifying what the extract is about, followed by several sentences briefly identifying its structure, that is, the different sections of the extract.)

The extract shows Shylock being taunted by Solanio and Salarino and exploring the motivation of his desired revenge against Antonio. When Tubal declares that he has been unable to track down Jessica, Shylock expresses his anger against his daughter. The extract has two sections. First, the Christians jibe at Shylock, twisting his words and mocking the loss of his daughter. Shylock, bruised by Jessica's betrayal, is further agitated about the growing likelihood that Antonio will be unable to repay his bond. He offers a moving plea for the common humanity of all people, but says that this justifies his instinct for revenge. Second, Shylock anguishes about his diminished wealth and how he would like to repay his daughter for what she has done. He feels increasingly alone and isolated.

**Paragraph 3: Identify the mood or atmosphere of the extract.**
The mood in the first section bristles with hostility and mistrust and is built on the tensions between Christian and Jew. Shylock appears more introspective and humane, but finally revengeful, as he painfully examines his feelings. He is torn between outrage and self-pity when he considers Jessica's deeds.

### Paragraph 4: Diction (vocabulary)

The Christians' delight in Shylock's discomfort is expressed through their punning responses to his loss. When Shylock speaks of Jessica's 'flight', Salarino twists the word into its literal meaning and talks of her 'wings'. Solanio visualises Jessica's departure as a bird leaving the 'dam' (mother) and Shylock joins in the sparring, using his own pun: 'She is damned for it.' When Shylock grieves over the way in which she could 'rebel', Solanio wilfully misinterprets Shylock as speaking of his inability to get an erection. Throughout the extract there is an association of devil and Jew, and both Shylock and Tubal are unnamed. The simple, concrete words of Shylock's 'plea' ('eyes', 'hands', 'organs', etc.) add to its emotional force. Shylock reminds the audience of the importance of his 'nation' and when Solanio describes Tubal as 'another of the tribe' the significance of their common Jewish identity is reiterated. The references to death ('hearsed', 'coffin') are an ominous reminder of the rift between Jessica and her father.

### Paragraph 5: Imagery

Jessica is portrayed as a bird that 'was fledged', a youngster who has left the domestic nest and the tight paternal control of Shylock. Shakespeare draws attention to Shylock's age and the contrast with the younger generation, stressing the difference between parent and child, when Solanio calls him 'old carrion' (a walking corpse). The Christians continue to underline the marked difference between Shylock and Jessica. She is 'ivory' to his 'jet' (black) and 'Rhenish' (fine wine) to his ordinary 'red wine'. Antonio is defined as a 'prodigal', confirming Shylock's contempt for his reckless waste of money. Shylock's urge to revenge is characterised as a hunger which he must 'feed', and his 'To bait fish withal' chillingly pictures his savage cruelty; 'hearsed at my foot' turns 'dead at my foot' into a vivid image of his malign intentions.

### Paragraph 6: Antithesis

Most of the extract is constructed around the difference between Christian and Jew and the conflict is powerfully expressed in antitheses : 'amen' and 'prayer' are set against 'devil'. Now that Jessica has eloped with Lorenzo she will convert to Christianity. She thus ceases to be Shylock's 'flesh and blood'. Shylock's loss of Jessica is set against Antonio's lost ship. Antonio's previous smugness about his mercantile successes is contrasted with his current situation as 'bankrupt' and 'beggar'. Shylock is the 'usurer'; Antonio lends money 'for a Christian courtesy' (without charge). Antonio's forfeited pound of flesh will literally act as fish food or it will feed Shylock's revenge. Shylock antithetically sets all he holds dear against Antonio's reaction: 'laughed' against 'losses'; 'mocked' against 'gains'; 'scorned' against 'nation'; 'cooled my friends' against 'heated mine enemies'. Shylock's anger vacillates between the loss of his daughter and the loss of his wealth. This is the moment in the play when Shylock addresses what he can gain from his loss.

### Paragraph 7: Repetition
Shylock's fixation that the Christians have conspired against him is encapsulated in his constant repetition. He accuses 'You knew, none so well, none so well as you . . .' and his loss is echoed in the repeated 'rebel'/'rebels' and 'flesh and blood'. His insistent 'Let him look to his bond' haunts the scene menacingly and is reaffirmed by the repetition of the word 'feed'. In order to emphasise his individual plight he reiterates the words 'me' and 'my' and the constant rhetorical questioning around the framework of 'Hath not . . .?' and 'If . . .?' draws attention to Shylock's frustration that Jews and Christians are not perceived as equals. Throughout the speech the word 'revenge' is emphatically repeated. In conversation with Tubal, Shylock focuses on the immediacy of his current predicament. The repeated phrase 'till now' hints that he has reached a defining moment in his suffering. His loss is emphasised through 'precious, precious jewels', 'loss upon loss' and 'so much'.

### Paragraph 8: Lists
Shylock's emotions are emphasised by the way he catalogues his feelings, piling item upon item. He scorns Antonio as 'another bad match: a bankrupt, a prodigal . . . a beggar'. He expresses his contempt towards Antonio in a blistering list of accusations concerning Antonio's actions: 'disgraced', 'hindered', 'laughed', 'mocked', 'scorned', 'thwarted', 'cooled', 'heated'. He characterises the common humanity of Jews in a long list of human endowments: 'Hath not a Jew hands, organs, dimensions, senses, affections, passions?' Shylock's frustration boils over in repeated negatives: 'no

satisfaction, no revenge, nor no ill luck stirring . . .' and his isolation is capped by 'no sighs but o'my breathing, no tears but o'my shedding!'

## Paragraph 9: Staging opportunities

The opening episode offers an opportunity to show once again Christian contempt for Jews. Salarino's controlled expression of sympathetic concern for Antonio's future is set against Shylock's dramatic entrance. He becomes very much a target of the Christians' abuse. Shylock's passionate language enables the actor to display a range of emotion. He might tick off his list on his fingers as he catalogues each of Antonio's offences against him. The public sparring can be replaced with a more introspective speech from Shylock. All productions have to decide whether he speaks to the Christians, to himself or directly to the audience. For example, his plea for understanding has added poignancy if addressed to the audience.

In the second part of the extract, when Shylock is with Tubal, the audience is offered a unique glimpse into the wider Jewish world within the play. Shylock's grief and pain are still acute, but Tubal can suggest a sense of brotherhood and share in Shylock's torment (although in one production, Tubal presented Shylock with a bill for his services during this scene).

## Paragraph 10: Conclusion

Many critics regard this scene as a pivotal one in terms of defining Shylock's intent to take revenge. Although there is debate about the moment when he makes up his mind (there may not even be a 'moment'), there is no doubt that the 'merry sport' of the bond has now become an earnest and deadly obsession. His intent is strengthened by the desertion of his daughter, increasing monetary losses and glimpses of Antonio's financial plight. The theme of revenge pulses dramatically through the extract and the tensions between Jew and Christian are powerfully explored. Shakespeare allows intimate insight into Shylock's state of mind. Although the extract is entirely in prose, the vitality, strength and passion of Shylock's language has similar intensity to verse and provides acute insight into his complex character. The scene is also an important bridge to the rest of the play. By the end of Act 3 Scene 1 Shylock has received more news of Antonio's losses and instructs Tubal to 'fee me an officer' to be ready to arrest Antonio.

## Reminders

- The framework is only a guide. It helps you to structure your writing. Use the framework for practice on other extracts. Adapt as you feel appropriate. Make it your own.
- Structure your response in paragraphs. Each paragraph makes a particular point and helps build up your argument.
- Focus tightly on the language, especially vocabulary, imagery, antithesis, lists, repetitions.
- Remember that *The Merchant of Venice* is a play, a drama intended for performance. The purpose of writing about an extract is to identify how Shakespeare creates dramatic effect. What techniques does he use?
- Try to imagine the action. Visualise the scene in your mind's eye. But remember there can be many valid ways of performing a scene. Offer alternatives. Justify your own preferences by reference to the language.
- Who is on stage? Imagine their interaction. How do 'silent characters' react to what's said?
- Look for the theatrical qualities of the extract. What guides for actors' movement and expressions are given in the language? Comment on any stage directions.
- How might the audience respond? In Elizabethan times? Today? How might you respond as a member of the audience?
- How might the lines be spoken? Tone, emphasis, pace, pauses? Identify shifting moods and registers. Is the verse pattern smooth or broken, flowing or full of hesitations and abrupt turns?
- What is the importance of the extract in the play as a whole? Justify its thematic significance.
- Are there 'key words'?
- How does the extract develop the plot, reveal character, deepen themes?
- In what ways can the extract be spoken/staged to reflect a particular interpretation?

# Writing an essay

As part of your study of *The Merchant of Venice* you will be asked to write essays, either under examination conditions or for coursework (term papers). Examinations mean that you are under pressure of time, usually having around one hour to prepare and write each essay. Coursework means that you have much longer to think about and produce your essay. But whatever the type of essay, each will require you to develop an argument about a particular aspect of *The Merchant of Venice*.

The essays you write on *The Merchant of Venice* require that you set out your thoughts on a particular aspect of the play, using evidence from the text. The people who read your essays (examiners, teachers, lecturers) will have certain expectations for your writing. In each essay they will expect you to discuss and analyse a particular topic, using evidence from the play to develop an argument in an organised, coherent and persuasive way. Examiners look for, and reward, what they call 'an informed personal response'. This simply means that you show you have good knowledge of the play ('informed') and can use evidence from it to support and justify your own viewpoint ('personal').

You can write about *The Merchant of Venice* from different points of view. As the Critical approaches section shows (pages 89–106), you can approach the play from a number of perspectives (feminist, political, psychoanalytic, etc.). You can also set the play in its social, literary, political and other contexts. You should write at different levels, moving beyond description to analysis and evaluation. Simply telling the story or describing characters is not as effective as analysing how events or characters embody wider concerns of the play (its themes, issues, preoccupations, or, more simply, 'what the play is about'). In *The Merchant of Venice*, these 'wider concerns' include prejudice, revenge, usury and commerce, patriarchy and women, friendship and love, justice and judgement.

How should you answer an examination question or write a coursework essay? The following threefold structure can help you organise your response:

opening paragraph
developing paragraphs
concluding paragraph.

*Opening paragraph.* Begin with a paragraph identifying just what topic or issue you will focus on. Show that you have understood what the question is about. You probably will have prepared for particular topics. But look closely at the question and identify key words to see what particular aspect it asks you to write about. Adapt your material to answer that question. Examiners do not reward an essay, however well written, if it is not on the question set.

*Developing paragraphs.* This is the main body of your essay. In it, you develop your argument, point by point, paragraph by paragraph. Use evidence from the play that illuminates the topic or issue, and answers the question set. Each paragraph makes a point of dramatic or thematic significance. Some paragraphs could make points concerned with context or particular critical approaches. The effect of your argument builds up as each paragraph adds to the persuasive quality of your essay. Use brief quotations that support your argument, and show clearly just why they are relevant. Ensure that your essay demonstrates that you are aware that *The Merchant of Venice* is a play; a drama intended for performance and, therefore, open to a wide variety of interpretations and audience responses.

*Concluding paragraph.* Your final paragraph pulls together your main conclusions. It does not simply repeat what you have written earlier, but summarises concisely how your essay has successfully answered the question.

## Example

The following notes show the 'ingredients' of an answer. In an examination it is usually helpful to prepare similar notes from which you write your essay, paragraph by paragraph. To help you understand how contextual matters or points from different critical approaches might be included, the words 'Context' or 'Criticism' appear before some items (but would not appear in your essay). Remember that examiners are not impressed by 'name-dropping': use of critics' names. They want you to show your own knowledge and judgement of the play and its contexts, and your understanding of how it has been interpreted from different critical perspectives.

Question: 'Consider the ways in which *The Merchant of Venice* explores the themes of love and hate.'

**Opening paragraph**

Show you are aware that the question asks you to display your understanding of the variety of ways Shakespeare presents and uses the themes of love and hate. Include the following points and aim to write a sentence or more on each:

- Criticism The play is built on a series of tensions, conflicts or oppositions (e.g. Jew/Christian, mercy/justice, father/daughter, usury/trade). Love and hate is one such tension.
- Criticism The conflicting themes of love and hate are central to the dramatic purpose of the play – and occur in different ways.
- The essay will first examine different kinds of love, then hate, then show how they deepen dramatic effect.

**Developing paragraphs**

Now write a paragraph on each of a number of different ways in which the theme of love might be defined. In each paragraph, identify the importance (dramatic, thematic, etc.) of the example you discuss. Follow this section with a number of paragraphs exploring the range of 'hate' in the play.

Different types of love

- Romantic. This focuses on the heightened, romantic nature of Bassanio's courtship of Portia. An example is the perplexing feelings of Portia (Act 3 Scene 2, lines 16–18), a woman in love and desperate to give herself to the man she desires. She later uses the words 'ecstasy' and 'joy'. A further example is Bassanio's praise of Portia after his casket choice: 'demi-god'; 'severed lips / Parted with sugar breath'; her hair described as 'A golden mesh'.
- Male/homoerotic friendship. Context This examines the (problematic?) relationship between Antonio and Bassanio. Antonio 'with affection wondrous sensible . . . wrung Bassanio's hand'. Solanio says of Antonio: 'I think he only loves the world for him'. Antonio urges Bassanio to 'Say how I loved you'.

- Friendship. Context Bassanio's friendship for Antonio can be viewed as typically Elizabethan (e.g. Bassanio says 'the dearest friend to me, the kindest man'; Portia urges him to 'bring your true friend along').
- Sexual. Criticism This paragraph acknowledges sexuality and desire. For example, the story of Lancelot and the Moor ('the getting up of the Negro's belly'); Gratiano's earthy coarseness ('stake down', meaning with a limp penis); the mention of 'Nerissa's ring' (female genitals); Portia's comment 'shall we turn to men?'
- Young love. The two eloping lovers ('Lorenzo and his amorous Jessica') exemplify this. Jessica flees from her father's control and converts to Christianity. Lorenzo speaks of Jessica: 'Beshrew me but I love her heartily.'
- Self-love. This is seen in the arrogance of Portia's suitors, Arragon and, in particular, Morocco ('I tell thee, lady, this aspèct of mine / Hath feared the valiant').
- Spiritual love. Bassanio emphasises Portia's spiritual qualities ('To kiss this shrine, this mortal breathing saint'). Portia 'kneels and prays / For happy wedlock hours'.
- Love of money. Criticism Characters are driven by financial motivation as well as romance. This is seen in the commercial language of Venice and Belmont, Shylock's usury ('well won thrift') and the bond. The courtship of Portia is presented in commercial terms ('a lady richly left'). Portia says 'I would be trebled twenty times myself' and 'the full sum of me / Is sum of something'.

Different types of hate
- Racial and tribal hatred. Context Portia draws on Elizabethan mistrust of foreigners and is overtly racist in dismissing her suitors ('Let all of his complexion choose me so').
- Racial hatred of Jews. Context The characters' hostility to Jews is explored in a variety of ways. Lancelot compares Shylock's Jewishness with 'devil'; Shylock talks of how Antonio 'hates our sacred nation'; Jessica is 'issue to a faithless Jew'.
- Racial hatred of Christians. Shylock expresses his enmity towards the Christians ('I hate him [Antonio] for he is a Christian').
- Verbal abuse. Hatred is expressed through verbal insults against Shylock: 'misbeliever', 'cut-throat dog', 'stranger cur', 'villain Jew', 'dog Jew', 'inhuman wretch', 'wolf', 'damned, inexecrable dog'.

- Hatred of the strictures of home. Context Jessica must rebel against her father ('Our house is hell'). Jessica is 'ashamed to be my father's child!' She smears her father's name: 'he would rather have Antonio's flesh'. She plunders his gold and jewels and wastes them frivolously.
- Hatred of merriment. Shylock's killjoy attitudes. He tells Jessica 'Lock up my doors'; he abjures 'shallow foppery' and 'fools with varnished faces'.
- Hatred expressed through revenge. Shylock turns his hatred back on his Christian tormentors ('I will feed fat the ancient grudge I bear him'; 'And if you wrong us, shall we not revenge?'; 'The villainy you teach me I will execute'; 'I would my daughter were dead at my foot').
- Hatred expressed through action. This is seen in the Christians' spitting, the way they 'rail' in public against Shylock, and Shylock's brandishing the knife in the trial.
- Hatred of deception. The Christians mistrust Shylock's motives. Bassanio is wary of Shylock ('I like not fair terms and a villain's mind'). Antonio reviles him (the 'villain with a smiling cheek'). Shylock's similar detestation ('How like a fawning publican he looks').

As you write, show awareness of:
- how Shakespeare dramatises the conflicting themes of love and hate. For example, Antonio's affection for Bassanio is the basis for the signing of the bond. It is that bond which feeds Shylock's impetus for revenge.
- how Shakespeare uses the themes of love and hate to increase dramatic tension. For example, in the trial scene, Antonio's selfless sacrifice is set against Shylock's selfish and ruthless pursuit of revenge.

### Concluding paragraph
Write several sentences pulling together your conclusions. You might include the following points:

- The balance between love (romance, affection and friendship, three marriages, selfless sacrifice) and hate (racist bullying, Shylock's rejection of his daughter, the pursuit of revenge).

- The way in which the two themes overlap uncomfortably (Shylock's love for his daughter and his wealth confirms his desire for revenge).
- The structure of the play. Shylock disappears in Act 4, and many critics see love replacing hate. Act 5 is full of comic and romantic moments, stories of great lovers, contests of wit, reconciliations, music, celebrations of marriage and the clearing up of mis-understandings.
- Criticism The polarised extremes of love and hate may suggest that the play does not fit snugly into one genre (e.g. comedy or romance).

## Writing about character

Much critical writing about *The Merchant of Venice* traditionally focused on characters, writing about them as if they were living human beings. Today it is not sufficient just to describe their personalities. When you write about characters you will also be expected to show that they are dramatic constructs, part of Shakespeare's stagecraft. They embody the wider concerns of the play, have certain dramatic functions, and are set in a social and political world with particular values and beliefs. They reflect and express issues of significance to Shakespeare's society – and today's.

All that may seem difficult and abstract. But don't feel over-whelmed. Everything you read in this book is written with those principles in mind, and can be a model for your own writing. Of course, you should say what a character seems like to you, but you should also write about how Shakespeare makes him or her part of his overall dramatic design. For example, Shakespeare creates dramatic patterns by making characters equivalent or contrasting in their dramatic functions:

- Both Portia and Jessica are victims of their fathers' patriarchal authority and control. Portia is constrained by the terms of her dead father's will and may not marry freely. Jessica, perhaps frustrated by her father's over-protectiveness, decides to convert to Christianity.
- Portia, Nerissa and Jessica all marry friends of Antonio. All are involved in the defeat of Shylock. All 'cross-dress' as men in order to effect that defeat.

- Antonio's sadness at the start of the play is contrasted directly with Portia's at the beginning of Act 1 Scene 2.
- Both Shylock and Jessica are excluded from Belmont. Shylock is never seen there. Jessica arrives at Belmont but seems largely ignored (whereas the Christians are welcomed, many by name). She is the 'stranger'.
- Antonio proposes himself twice in a bond on Bassanio's behalf: once to Shylock in the 'pound of flesh' bond and then to Portia in Act 5 when he declares 'I dare be bound again' as a pledge that Bassanio will not break his matrimonial oath to Portia.

A different way of thinking of characters is that in Shakespeare's time, playwrights and audiences were less concerned with psychological realism than with character types and their functions. That is, they expected and recognised such stock figures of traditional drama as the avaricious, possessive father figure (Shylock), the beautiful daughter who needs to rebel and escape from a repressive home life (Jessica) and the attractive, clever young man who orchestrates her escape (Lorenzo).

Today, film and television have accustomed audiences to expect the inner life of characters to be revealed. Although Shakespeare's characters do reveal their inmost thoughts and feelings, especially in soliloquy, his audiences tended to regard them as characters in a developing story, to be understood by how they formed part of that story, and by how far they conformed to certain well-known types and fulfilled certain traditional roles.

But there is also a danger in writing about the functions of characters or the character types they represent. To reduce a character to a mere plot device is just as inappropriate as treating him or her as a real person. When you write about characters in *The Merchant of Venice* you should try to achieve a balance between analysing their personality, identifying the dilemmas they face, and placing them in their social, critical and dramatic contexts. That style of writing is found all through this guide, and that, together with the following brief discussions, can help your own written responses to character.

## Shylock
In the Elizabethan theatre, Shylock was performed to match the way he is described by his Christian enemies. He was presented as a comic

villain, grotesque, outrageously caricatured as the miserly money-lender. He later became evil and terrifying, a villain who was incapable of humour and who was stubborn, malicious and threatening.

In the nineteenth century, Edmund Kean broke away from this traditionally accepted way of portraying Shylock and developed him as an intelligent and vulnerable character whose dignity and isolation made him increasingly sympathetic. Shylock's pleas for humanity and understanding became central in performance. Emphasis on his 'Hath not a Jew eyes?' speech softened the harshness and repellence which had earlier characterised him. This changed him from a comic character to much more of a tragic one. He became less of a villain, more of a victim, whose hatred and desire for revenge exposed the injustice and intolerance of the society in which he lived.

More recent critical character studies (such as that by James Shapiro) have explored his usury and his Jewish background more fully and placed his Jewishness (and the symbolism of his 'flesh-cutting') at the heart of his conflict with the Christians. He is widely viewed as a foreigner, an outsider, even an alien within the social context of the play. He is seen as vital to the play's exploration of religious and cultural identity, and is central to the play's moral impact.

## Antonio

Antonio is the merchant of the play's title (although an eighteenth-century version of the play renamed it *The Jew of Venice*). Traditional criticism considered him as an affluent gentleman, at ease within refined social and economic circles, very much associated with the values supposedly represented by Venice. Antonio is generous to Bassanio but loathes Shylock. Until the twentieth century, his loneliness and sadness were not attributed to his homoerotic feelings for Bassanio. More recently, critics such as Graham Midgley have been explicit: 'Antonio is an outsider because he is an unconscious homosexual in a predominantly, and indeed blatantly, heterosexual society'.

## Portia

Most criticism points to the inconsistencies in Portia's presentation. She has many seemingly paradoxical identities:

- the dutiful daughter, compliant to her father's will
- the innocent young woman ('unlessoned . . . unschooled, unpractised')
- the 'mortal-breathing saint' who possesses 'god-like amity'
- the hard-hearted and calculating lawyer who is fully conversant with the tricks of the legal trade
- the advocate of mercy who ruthlessly destroys Shylock
- the innocent virgin who knows all about male sexuality
- the racist mocker of the suitors she finds unfavourable
- the wealthy and independent woman who nevertheless gives herself willingly to her husband's authority
- the mocking, teasing and barbed tormentor of her husband in the 'rings' test

Some modern criticism highlights her willingness to embrace racist attitudes. It rejects Portia as an innocent, virtuous 'Victorian' heroine. She is seen as a devious manipulator, who subverts the meaning of what she says. She is fundamental to the preservation of the values and beliefs of the male world of Venice (and Belmont). But some feminist criticism argues that she stands for female resistance in a male world, showing herself able to take on, and defeat, men at their own game (winning in the law court and using the 'rings' test to establish control over her husband).

# A note on examiners

Examiners do not try to trap you or trick you. They set questions and select passages for comment intended to help you write your own informed personal response to the play. They expect your answer to display a sound knowledge and understanding of the play, and to be well structured. They want you to develop an argument, using evidence from the text to support your interpretations and judgements. Examiners know there is never one 'right answer' to a question, but always opportunities to explore different approaches and interpretations. As such, they welcome answers which directly address the question set, and which demonstrate originality, insight and awareness of complexity. Above all, they reward responses which show your awareness that *The Merchant of Venice* is a play for performance, and that you can identify how Shakespeare achieves his dramatic effects.

And what about critics? Examiners want you to show you are aware of different critical approaches to the play. But they do not expect you simply to drop critics' names into your essay, or to remember quotations from critics. Rather, they want you to show that you can interpret the play from different critical perspectives, and that you know that any critical approach provides only a partial view of *The Merchant of Venice*. Often, that need only be just a part of your essay. Examiners are always interested in your view of the play. They expect your writing to show how you have come to that view from thinking critically about the play, reading it, seeing it performed, reading about it, and perhaps from acting some of it yourself – even if that acting takes place in your imagination!

# Resources

## Books

**Catherine Belsey**, 'Love in Venice', in Martin Coyle (ed.), *New Casebooks: The Merchant of Venice*, Macmillan, 1998

**Harold Bloom**, *Shakespeare: The Invention of the Human*, Fourth Estate, 1999
Bloom's book is censured by most critics. But his chapter on *The Merchant of Venice* is full of lively and provocative judgements to test against your own responses.

**A C Bradley**, *Shakespearean Tragedy*, Penguin, 1991
Originally published in 1904, this is the most important source of 'character criticism' (but *Merchant* is not discussed).

**John Russell Brown**, *Shakespeare and his Comedies*, Methuen, 1962
An accessible study of the play which looks at key thematic issues.

**James C Bulman**, *Shakespeare in Performance: The Merchant of Venice*, Manchester University Press, 1991
Discussion of major productions from Henry Irving's in 1879 to the BBC television version in 1980; reveals great variation in interpretation and performance.

**Martin Coyle** (ed.), *New Casebooks: The Merchant of Venice*, Macmillan, 1998
A valuable collection of modern criticism (contains the articles by Belsey, Newman, Hall and Sinfield noted in this book list).

**Lawrence Danson**, *The Harmonies of The Merchant of Venice*, Yale University Press, 1978
A detailed examination of 'ironic' and 'idealistic' interpretations of the play. Danson favours the latter approaches, arguing that the play is a romantic comedy and ends in complex harmonies.

**Harley Granville-Barker**, *Prefaces to Shakespeare: Love's Labour's Lost, Romeo and Juliet, The Merchant of Venice*, Batsford, 1982
A highly influential reading by a theatre practitioner. Essential for students of stagecraft. Extracts reprinted in John Widers' *The Merchant of Venice: A Casebook* (see below).

**John Gross**, *Shylock: Four Hundred Years in the Life of a Legend*, Chatto and Windus, 1992
A very readable account of Shakespeare's Shylock: his origins, how he has been performed and written about over the centuries, and his cultural stereotyping as a symbol of capitalism and anti-Semitism.

**Kim F Hall**, 'Guess Who's Coming to Dinner? Colonialisation and Miscegenation in *The Merchant of Venice*', in Martin Coyle (ed.), *New Casebooks: The Merchant of Venice*, Macmillan, 1998

**Graham Holderness**, *The Merchant of Venice*, Penguin, 1993
A reading of the play which examines the complexities of trying to define its genre and how a modern reception is coloured by the Holocaust.

**Norman N Holland**, *Psychoanalysis and Shakespeare*, McGraw Hill, 1964
A mid-twentieth-century survey of psychoanalytic approaches to all Shakespeare's plays. The dozen pages on *Merchant* provide a fascinating range of interpretations.

**John Lyon**, *Harvester New Critical Introductions to Shakespeare: The Merchant of Venice*, Harvester Wheatsheaf, 1988
A valuable introduction to a range of critical issues that the play has provoked.

**Graham Midgley**, '*The Merchant of Venice*: A Reconsideration', in John Wilders (ed.), *The Merchant of Venice: A Casebook*, Macmillan, 1969

**A D Moody**, *Shakespeare: The Merchant of Venice*, Arnold, 1964
A brief but useful introduction that argues the play is deeply ironic, presenting both Jew and Christian as unpleasant characters.

**Karen Newman**, 'Portia's Ring: Unruly Women and Structures of Exchange in *The Merchant of Venice*', in Martin Coyle (ed.), *New Casebooks: The Merchant of Venice*, Macmillan, 1998

**Kiernan Ryan**, *Shakespeare (2nd edition)*, Harvester Wheatsheaf, 1995
Ryan argues that *The Merchant of Venice* explores the conflict between 'racist capitalism and humanity'.

**James Shapiro**, *Shakespeare and the Jews*, Columbia University Press, 1996
A very full account of the history of Jews in England, showing how the play reflects the fantasies, anxieties and pleasures of Shakespeare's audiences.

**Alan Sinfield**, 'How to Read *The Merchant of Venice* without being Heterosexist', in Martin Coyle (ed.), *New Casebooks: The Merchant of Venice*, Macmillan, 1998

**Caroline Spurgeon**, *Shakespeare's Imagery and What it Tells Us*, Cambridge University Press, 1935
The first major study of imagery in the plays. Spurgeon's identification of image-clusters as a dominant feature of the plays has influenced later studies.

**John Wilders** (ed.), *The Merchant of Venice: A Casebook*, Macmillan, 1969
A valuable collection of extracts from criticism up to 1963. (Contains criticism by Granville-Barker and Midgley discussed in this guide.)

# Films

*The Merchant of Venice* has rarely been filmed, although there are three relatively recent film versions which are usually available on video or DVD (but distributors sometimes restrict availability in certain countries).

- *The Merchant of Venice* (UK, 1969). Director: Jonathan Miller. Laurence Olivier (Shylock). The production is set around the close of the nineteenth century and reflects Victorian elegance. Venice and Belmont are portrayed as worlds of opulence and privilege. The Christians are aristocratic gentry; Shylock is both socially and culturally assimilated.
- *The Merchant of Venice* (UK, 1980). Director: Jack Gold. Warren Mitchell (Shylock). This television production stresses the 'alien' nature of Shylock by presenting him as an ethnic Jew. His Jewishness is emphasised by his appearance, his accent and his mannerisms. The enclosed world of Venice is contrasted with the airy spaciousness of Belmont.
- *The Merchant of Venice* (UK, 2001). Director: Trevor Nunn. Henry Goodman (Shylock). This production transfers the action to the early 1930s and suggests a German location for the play. This setting draws audience attention to features of Nazi Germany and the impending Holocaust. The portrayal of Shylock shows how he has been affected by vicious abuse, both for his religion and his means of earning a living.

# Audio books

Three major versions are easily available, in the series produced by:

Arkangel (Shylock: Trevor Peacock)
BBC Radio Collection (Shylock: Warren Mitchell)
Harper Collins (Shylock: Hugh Griffiths)

## *The Merchant of Venice* on the Web

If you type 'The Merchant of Venice' into your search engine, it will find nearly 76,000 items. Because websites are of wildly varying quality, and rapidly disappear or are created, no recommendation can safely be made. But if you have time to browse, you may find much of interest.